YORK NOTES

POWER AND CONFLICT

AQA POETRY ANTHOLOGY

NOTES BY BETH KEMP

Pearson

YORK PRESS

YORK PRESS
322 Old Brompton Road, London SW5 9JH

PEARSON EDUCATION LIMITED
Edinburgh Gate, Harlow,
Essex CM20 2JE, United Kingdom
Associated companies, branches and representatives throughout the world

First published 2017

10 9 8 7 6 5 4

ISBN 978–1–2922–3031–3

Phototypeset by DTP Media
Printed in Slovakia

Text credits: 'Storm on the Island' from *Poems 1965–1975* by Seamus Heaney. Copyright © 1980 by
Seamus Heaney. Reprinted by permission of Farrar, Straus and Giroux and of Faber and Faber Ltd.
'Bayonet Charge' from *Collected Poems* by Ted Hughes. Copyright © 2003 by The Estate of Ted Hughes.
Reprinted by permission of Farrar, Straus and Giroux and of Faber and Faber Ltd. 'Remains' by Simon
Armitage from *The Not Dead*, 2008, published by Pomona, reproduced by kind permission of Pomona.
'Poppies' by Jane Weir: Copyright Templar Poetry from *The Way I Dressed During the Revolution*
(Templar, 2010). 'War Photographer' from *Standing Female* Nude by Carol Ann Duffy. Published by
Anvil Press Poetry, 1985. Copyright © Carol Ann Duffy. Reproduced by permission of the author c/o
Rogers, Coleridge & White Ltd., 20 Powis Mews, London W11 1JN. 'Tissue' by Imtiaz Dharker from *The
terrorist at my table* (Bloodaxe Books, 2006) reprinted with permission of Bloodaxe Books on behalf
of the author. www.bloodaxebooks.com. 'The Emigrée' by Carol Rumens reproduced by permission of
the author. 'Checking Out Me History' copyright © 1996 by John Agard reproduced by kind permission
of John Agard c/o Caroline Sheldon Literary Agency Ltd. 'Kamikaze' by Beatrice Garland: Copyright
Templar Poetry from *The Invention of Fireworks* (Templar, 2013).

Photo credits: Graficam Ahmed Saeed/Shutterstock for page 9 / Kochneva Tetyana/Shutterstock for
page 10 / AC Rider/Shutterstock for page 12 / Lefter is Papaulakis/Shutterstock for page 13 top / Katja
Wickert/Shutterstock for page 13 middle / Stewart Smith Photography/Shutterstock for page 16 / NEIL
ROY JOHNSON/Shutterstock for page 17 / pavel068/Shutterstock for page 20 / Janusz Pienkowski/
Shutterstock for page 21 top / Print Collector/Hulton Archive/Getty for page 21 bottom / Tony Baggett/
Shutterstock.com for page 24 / Mega Pixel/Shutterstock for page 25 / aarrows/Shutterstock for
page 28 / MSK Photography/Shutterstock for page 29 / Lee Caine/Shutterstock for page 31 / Helen
Hotson/Shutterstock for page 32 top / Gabor Kovacs Photography/Shutterstock for page 32 bottom
/ Inge Jansen/Shutterstock for page 34 / Grisha Bruev/Shutterstock for page 35 / Angela N Perryman/
Shutterstock.com for page 37/ Cameron Watson/Shutterstock for page 38 / WILLSIE/Shutterstock for
page 40 / Kuttelvaserova Stuchelova/Shutterstock for page 41 / albinoni/Shutterstock for page 43 /
Tomas Urbelionis/Shutterstock for page 44 / ZoriaOleksandra/Shutterstock for page 47 / Fer Gregory/
Shutterstock for page 48 / upslim/Shutterstock for page 50 / nature10/Shutterstock for page 51 / tomazi/
iStock for page 54 / Peshkova/Shutterstock for page 55 / Zhukov/Shutterstock for page 58 / Rich Carey/
Shutterstock for page 59 / Photology1971/Shutterstock for page 60 / Sariana/Shutterstock for page 61 /
DEA/G.NIMATALLAH/Contributor De Agostini Editorial/Getty for page 62 / mattomedia Werbeagentur/
Shutterstock for page 64 / Nataly Lukhanina/Shutterstock for page 65 / martan/Shutterstock for page
66 / Kadak/Shutterstock for page 67 / Andrey Kozachenko/Shutterstock for page 68 middle / RapidEye/
iStock for page 68 bottom / Corepics VOF/Shutterstock for page 69 / My Good Images/Shutterstock for
page 70 top / Jan van der Hoeven/Shutterstock for page 70 bottom / Print Collector/Contributor Hulton
Archive/Getty for page 71 / Mikhail_Kayl/Shutterstock for page 73 / Gino Santa Maria/Shutterstock
for page 74 / Wire_man/Shutterstock for page 75 / Polarpx/Shutterstock for page 76 / Radoslaw/
Shutterstock for page 77 / Federico Rostagno/Shutterstock for page 78 / Siwabud Veerapaisarn/
Shutterstock for page 79 / Nook Thitipat/Shutterstock for page 80 / Matt Gibson/Shutterstock for page
81 / ventdusud/Shutterstock for page 82 / ch123/Shutterstock for page 83

CONTENTS

PART FOUR:
FORM, STRUCTURE AND LANGUAGE

PART FIVE:
COMPARING POEMS IN THE CLUSTER

PART SIX:
APPROACHING 'UNSEEN' POEMS

PART SEVEN:
PROGRESS BOOSTER ★

PART EIGHT:
FURTHER STUDY AND ANSWERS

PART ONE: GETTING STARTED

PREPARING FOR ASSESSMENT

HOW WILL I BE ASSESSED ON MY WORK ON *POWER AND CONFLICT?*

When studying the cluster, your work will be examined through these three Assessment Objectives:

Assessment Objectives	Wording	Worth thinking about ...
AO1	Read, understand and respond to texts. Students should be able to: ● maintain a critical style and develop an informed personal response ● use textual references, including quotations, to support and illustrate interpretations.	● How well do I know what happens, what people say, do, etc., in each poem? ● What do *I* think about the key ideas in the poems? ● How can I support my viewpoint in a really convincing way? ● What are the best quotations to use and when should I use them?
AO2	Analyse the language, form and structure used by a writer to create meanings and effects, using relevant subject terminology where appropriate.	● What specific things do the poets 'do'? What choices has each poet made? (Why this particular word, phrase or image here? Why does this change occur at this point?) ● What effects do these choices create? (Suspense? Sympathy? Awe?)
AO3 *	Show understanding of the relationships between texts and the contexts in which they were written.	● What can I learn about society from the poems? (What do they tell me about justice and prejudice, for example?) ● What was/is society like for the poets? Can I see it reflected in their poems?

*AO3 is only assessed in relation to the cluster, and not in relation to the 'unseen' part of the exam (see **Part Six: Approaching 'unseen' poems**).

In other parts of your English Literature GCSE a fourth Assessment Objective, **AO4**, which is related to spelling, punctuation and grammar, is also assessed. While you will not gain any marks for AO4 in your poetry examination, it is still important to ensure that you write accurately and clearly, in order to get your points across to the examiner in the best possible way.

Look out for the Assessment Objective labels throughout your York Notes Study Guide – these will help to focus your study and revision!

The text used in this Study Guide is *Past and Present: Poetry Anthology* (AQA, 2015).

HOW TO USE YOUR YORK NOTES STUDY GUIDE

In this York Notes Study Guide you will find the text of every poem in the cluster, fully annotated, plus over 20 pages of detailed analysis of themes, contexts, structure, form and language. There are special sections on Comparing poems and the Unseen part of your exam, three sample practice papers, and annotated sample answers at three different levels.

So how will these Notes help you study and revise? Here are some suggestions:

- **A step-by-step study and revision guide** – work through the poems in Part Two to help you study them, then use the analysis sections to focus your learning. Finally hone your exams skills and practise for the exam.

- **A 'dip-in' support** – know the cluster quite well already but want to check your understanding and practise your skills? Look for the section you think you need most help with and go for it!

- **A revision guide before your exam** – use Parts Two to Four to check your knowledge, then work through Parts Five to Eight as you revise for your exam.

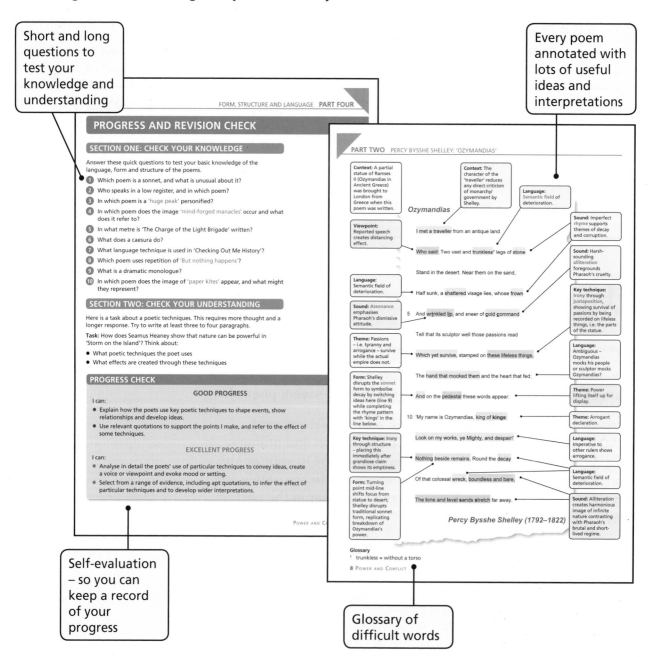

Short and long questions to test your knowledge and understanding

Every poem annotated with lots of useful ideas and interpretations

Self-evaluation – so you can keep a record of your progress

Glossary of difficult words

HOW TO READ AND STUDY A POEM

When you read and study a poem, or a set of poems, there are a number of key areas you will need to explore. These will ensure you enjoy your reading and study, and equally importantly, engage with the poem so that you can respond intelligently and thoughtfully.

KEY ASPECTS TO CONSIDER

As with any text, the secret to exploring the poem on the page in front of you is to consider its ingredients: the particular elements that create meaning or impact on you as a reader.

These will include:

1. What the **narrative** of the poem is – its story, or the experience it describes
   For example, does the poem describe something particular that happens? Is it a personal story or a public one? What actually happens? (Sometimes poems don't seem to tell a story at all, but all poems are about *something,* however small or apparently insignificant.)

2. The voice (or voices) and viewpoint
   For example, does the poem seem to be 'told' to us by one specific person or speaker? Is it a conversation? Some poems have a speaker who addresses us directly, while others maintain a more neutral or authoritative voice.

3. The **'message'** and/or **theme** of the poem – its concerns
   For example, does the poem explicitly direct the reader to consider a particular issue? Are there questions that it raises? This aspect is related to the poem's topic or subject, but is a broader issue – usually something more universal.

4. The poem's distinctive **language features**, or **poetic techniques** used by the poet
   For example, how is the poem written? Does it use rich imagery? Everyday language? Are there significant semantic fields, patterns of rhyme, rhythm, alliteration? (And, of course: what is the effect of this?)

5. The poem's structure and **organisation**
   repetition
   For example, is the poem organised into stanzas? Is there a chronological or other order to the information we are given? How are sentence and line lengths used?

6. The **opening** and **ending**
   For example, what is the impact of the poem's opening? Is there repetition or some kind of balance in how the poem opens and closes? Does the ending change our understanding of earlier lines?

7. **Patterns** of **sound** and **rhythm**
   For example, does the poet use repeated rhythms, rhyming patterns or use alliteration and assonance in a repeated or patterned way? What is the impact of these patterns – or lack of pattern?

8. **Contexts** and **settings**
   For example, what might have been the poet's background or influences? Can you infer any influences from the time the poem was written or where the poem 'takes place' (if relevant)?

TOP TIP (A01)

Always read a poem at least twice before you begin writing about it. On your first reading you are likely to get a general impression of the poem's tone and what it is about. On your second reading try to focus on the rhythm and language choices and you should find the meaning becomes clearer and you start to notice the poet's techniques and their effects.

Context: A partial statue of Ramses II (Ozymandias in Ancient Greece) was brought to London from Greece when this poem was written.

Context: The character of the 'traveller' reduces any direct criticism of monarchy/government by Shelley.

Language: Semantic field of deterioration.

Ozymandias

Viewpoint: Reported speech creates distancing effect.

Sound: Imperfect rhyme supports themes of decay and corruption.

I met a traveller from an antique land

Who said: Two vast and trunkless¹ legs of stone

Sound: Harsh-sounding alliteration foregrounds Pharaoh's cruelty.

Stand in the desert. Near them on the sand,

relating to meaning

Language: Semantic field of deterioration.

Half sunk, a shattered visage lies, whose frown

facial features

Key technique: Irony through juxtaposition, showing survival of passions by being recorded on lifeless things, i.e. the parts of the statue.

Sound: Assonance emphasises Pharaoh's dismissive attitude.

5   And wrinkled lip, and sneer of cold command

Tell that its sculptor well those passions read

Theme: Passions – i.e. tyranny and arrogance – survive while the actual empire does not.

Which yet survive, stamped on these lifeless things,

Language: Ambiguous – Ozymandias mocks his people or sculptor mocks Ozymandias?

The hand that mocked them and the heart that fed;

Form: Shelley disrupts the sonnet form to symbolise decay by switching ideas here (line 9) while completing the rhyme pattern with 'kings' in the line below.

And on the pedestal these words appear:

Theme: Power lifting itself up for display.

10   'My name is Ozymandias, king of **kings**:

Theme: Arrogant declaration.

Key technique: Irony through structure – placing this immediately after grandiose claim shows its emptiness.

Look on my works, ye Mighty, and despair!'

Language: Imperative to other rulers shows arrogance.

Nothing beside remains. Round the decay

Language: Semantic field of deterioration.

Form: Turning point mid-line shifts focus from statue to desert; Shelley disrupts traditional sonnet form, replicating breakdown of Ozymandias's power.

Of that colossal wreck, boundless and bare,

The lone and level sands stretch far away.

Sound: Alliteration creates harmonious image of infinite nature contrasting with Pharaoh's brutal and short-lived regime.

Percy Bysshe Shelley (1792–1822)

Glossary
¹ trunkless = without a torso

SUMMARY

- The speaker retells a conversation with a traveller about an old, broken statue in the desert.
- The traveller describes two legs and a powerful-looking, disdainful face.
- The statue's pedestal says it is of 'Ozymandias, king of kings' (10) and bids the onlooker – and especially other kings – to admire his works and 'despair' (11).
- The ending describes the barrenness of the desert around the broken statue.

KEY ASPECTS OF THE POEM

A   The use of the **traveller** to describe the statue **distances** the reader from the poem's original speaker. This sense of distance supports the poem's ancient subject matter, while the **reported speech** element helps to make the views expressed seem **universal** and **absolute**.

B   Shelley's use of irony contrasts the arrogance of the inscription with the actual physical state of the statue, showing how **worldly power** crumbles and fades.

C   'Ozymandias' is a sonnet in pentameter using rhyme. This form gives it weight and a serious tone.

KEY CONTEXT **A03**

Shelley (1792–1822) was a Romantic poet well known for his radical and anti-establishment ideas. He came from a wealthy Sussex family, attended Eton and was disinherited after being expelled from Oxford University for writing about atheism.
'Ozymandias' can be seen as a political statement against any one person or group gaining great power and wealth, and shows that such power can be lost.

KEY SETTING: THE EGYPTIAN DESERT (A03)

Ozymandias was the Ancient Greek name for the Egyptian Pharaoh Ramses II. The poem was inspired by the removal of parts of a statue from a temple in Greece to the British Museum at the time Shelley was writing. The great riches and advanced civilisation of Ancient Egypt are well known still, and yet the actual power associated with this culture has long since disappeared.

Shelley depicts the desert as a barren wasteland, which may symbolically represent the pointlessness of great empires. Another aspect of the setting is the framing device: the way the poem is effectively all reported speech from 'a traveller' (1). Almost as a final insult, Ozymandias, 'king of kings' (10), is further reduced to being just a story passed around in chance encounters, and we don't know where the poem's speaker is or where the meeting took place.

KEY TECHNIQUE: IRONY (A02)

Shelley uses irony to enable the reader to share his criticism of Ozymandias, and perhaps also of other all-powerful regimes. Despite Ozymandias's statement about his 'works' (11), nothing is left now except the statue, which makes the boastful comment ironic, and highlights how wrong Ozymandias was to make such bold claims.

Shelley also creates irony through **juxtaposition**: by placing Ozymandias's grand claims so physically close in the poem to the simple sentence 'Nothing beside remains' (12). This statement reveals the king's boasts to be ironic in their inaccuracy and makes them – and him – ridiculous.

The timing of this within the poem as a whole is also highly effective, as it follows the detailed description of how the sculptor has portrayed Ozymandias's attitude in his physical appearance. Shelley builds up the reader's sense of the king's arrogance gradually before presenting the inscription. Finally the emptiness of the desert is emphasised through two pairs of **adjectives** linked by **alliteration**: 'boundless and bare' (14) and 'lone and level' (15).

CHECKPOINT 1 (A01)

What does 'visage' (4) mean?

facial features/
expression

TOP TIP: WRITING ABOUT SHELLEY'S USE OF THE SONNET FORM (A02)

Sonnets can usually be separated into distinct sections according to their rhyme schemes: generally a block of eight lines followed by one of six with different rhyming patterns. Shelley, however, disrupts this pattern in 'Ozymandias' by continuing the rhymes of the octave into the sestet and only gradually introducing new ones. This is highly unusual, to the extent that this poem is often cited as an exception in critical works on sonnet forms. The metre and rhyme scheme Shelley uses in 'Ozymandias' is unique, which fits with the poem's exotic subject matter. Many critics see Shelley's subversion of the sonnet form here as deliberate, as his way of representing the decay and breakdown of both Ozymandias's power and the civilisation he ruled in the very structure of the poem.

Voice: Anonymous first person speaker walks without purpose through the city.

Form: Regular iambic pentameter mimics natural speech.

Sound: Regular alternate rhyme runs throughout entire poem, perhaps echoing drudgery and inevitability of ordinary life.

Theme: Poem expresses frustration at people owning every aspect of the city, even the river.

Language: Repetition of the word 'mark' using different meanings (to notice, sign/scar) emphasises the effect on both the speaker and the people he observes.

Key technique: Metaphor conveys entrapment in psychological chains created and maintained by ideas/beliefs.

Sound: Sibilance presents soldier (like all people in the poem) as powerless through his sigh.

Key technique: Use of the definite article helps create archetype rather than individual character to show universality.

Language: Plosive alliterated verbs imply violence.

Language: Oxymoron links death to marriage, which would traditionally be seen as having the function of producing children.

Theme: Everyone in the city is affected and 'stained' by misery.

Language: Repetition of 'every' highlights universal effects of oppression.

Context: In eighteenth-century London, child labour was common and chimney-sweepers struggled due to poverty and oppression.

Context: Colours of red and black refer to the French Revolution and may imply that London could also revolt against the institutions of Church and State (i.e. the Palace).

Context: The young prostitute's curse is juxtaposed with the baby's cry below, suggesting the corruption of innocence.

Form: Blake uses regular rhyme and rhythm as this is a song produced for the collection *Songs of Experience*.

London

I wander through each chartered street,

Near where the chartered Thames does flow,

And mark in every face I meet

Marks of weakness, marks of woe.

5   In every cry of every man,

In every infant's cry of fear,

In every voice, in every ban,

The mind-forged manacles I hear:

How the chimney-sweeper's cry

10 Every black'ning church appalls,

And the hapless soldier's sigh

Runs in blood down palace walls.

But most through midnight streets I hear

How the youthful harlot's curse

15 Blasts the new-born infant's tear,

And blights with plagues the marriage hearse.

William Blake (1757–1827)

chartered: qualified as a member of a professional body that has a royal charter

KEY CONTEXT **A03**

Blake (1757–1827) is regarded as a Romantic poet, and as a radical and mystic thinker. He worked as an engraver and was not well known as a poet during his lifetime. He believed strongly in the idea of revolution, seeing rebellion against oppression as inevitable but also as morally right. 'London' summarises his frustrations about his beloved home city, which he saw as corrupted by greed and inequality.

KEY CONTEXT **A03**

A charter grants rights of ownership and use. Blake felt that charters gave rights only to the wealthy, often allowing people and companies to own and control land and resources which previously had not been privately owned but had been available for the public to use.

SUMMARY

- The speaker notices how oppressed people in London have become now that everything is 'chartered' (1–2).
- This is apparent in all kinds of people, who are trapped in the symbolic chains referred to as 'mind-forged manacles' (8).
- The speaker refers to child workers and soldiers, and connects them to institutions such as the church and the 'palace' (12), both of which are presented as dramatically stained.
- Finally, the speaker reflects on the pitiful state of the streets at night, linking the ideas of prostitutes, new-born babies, disease, marriage and death.

KEY ASPECTS OF THE POEM

A The repetition in the first half of the poem is a key language technique, emphasising the speaker's initial **unhappiness** with the situation in London and building up to a strong picture of universal **oppression** with the **five-fold repetition** of 'every' (5–10).

B Blake uses a regular **rhythm** and **rhyme** scheme. The poem comes from his collection *Songs of Innocence and of Experience*, so a **song-like feel** is appropriate. This is an 'Experience' poem, giving a more **mature** and more **pessimistic** view of the world.

C Some of Blake's **vocabulary choices** are worth noting. The **verbs** 'forged' (8), 'appalls' (10), 'blasts' (15) and 'blights' (16) are all forceful, which contributes to the poem's increasingly **violent tone**.

KEY SETTING: LONDON   **A03**

Eighteenth-century London was developing rapidly under industrialisation, which resulted in considerable poverty and extremely poor living conditions. Child labour was commonplace, and poorer children in particular worked long hours in dangerous environments. Blake's poem outlines his concerns about Londoners' lack of personal freedom by underscoring the way the city was being controlled by charters at the time, and suggesting that even the river Thames was controlled by the powerful.

KEY THEME: OPPRESSION   **A02**

Blake states that everyone he sees is affected by 'weakness' and 'woe' (4) but selects some particular victims of oppression to draw attention to in the poem. He singles out infants, chimney-sweepers, soldiers and prostitutes as individuals, all of whom can be seen as powerless in their specific contexts. For each of these, he uses a phrase with the definite article 'the' (9, 11, 14, 15) to make an individual into an archetype, so that they symbolise their whole profession or age. It is also worth noting that Blake pairs his comments on the sweeper and the soldier with the 'church' and the 'palace', implicating the institutions they represent in the oppression of these individuals.

KEY CONTEXT: THE FRENCH REVOLUTION (A03)

Blake was known to be a supporter of the French Revolution and wore a red hat known as a Phrygian cap or *bonnet rouge* in the streets in the year when he was writing 'London'. These caps had been given to freed slaves by Ancient Romans to mark their new liberty and were therefore a powerful symbol of freedom. At its root, the French Revolution was about the oppression of the people as the aristocracy sought more power and wealth. Blake's poem alludes to this in the 'blood' running down 'palace walls' (12) and some consider that he is implying here that revolution could also happen in England. Red and black in French culture symbolise the institutions of the military (red) and the Church (black) because of the colours of their uniforms.

1789
1989

KEY QUOTATION: TRAPPED BY FALSE CHAINS (A02)

The phrase 'mind-forged manacles' (8) is perhaps the most famous from this poem and has been discussed by many critics, owing to its ambiguity. Both the **noun** 'mind' and the verb 'forged' can be interpreted in more than one way, although the overall interpretation remains the same: the people of London are enslaved by chains which are not physically real, but are products of the imagination. The use of the word 'manacles' invokes the idea of slavery.

Blake may be implying that other minds have created these manacles, or that people have internalised the oppression and are now effectively holding themselves hostage. Either interpretation of 'mind' is supported by the poem. Equally, the verb 'forged' seems to refer to blacksmithing, producing

manacles from iron, while at the same time perhaps making the reader think of forgery, of manacles that are fake or untrue.

REVISION FOCUS: EXPLORING THE PRESENTATION OF OPPRESSION

Working through the cluster as a whole, select the poems which discuss the theme of oppression. Create a mind map, table or other diagram to help you compare **how** they present this theme, focusing on the language and poetic techniques used to do this, and their effects. This will help you to get to know the poems and is useful practice for how you need to work in the exam, where you should compare how poets present ideas.

KEY CONTEXT (A03)

The French Revolution came about largely because of a sense of great inequality between classes. Lower classes revolted against injustice and eventually attacked the centres of power: the aristocracy, the monarchy and the Church. This resulted in the end of a monarchy in France with the execution of Louis XVI in January 1793, followed by the Reign of Terror, when many men and women were executed by guillotine, including Queen Marie Antoinette.

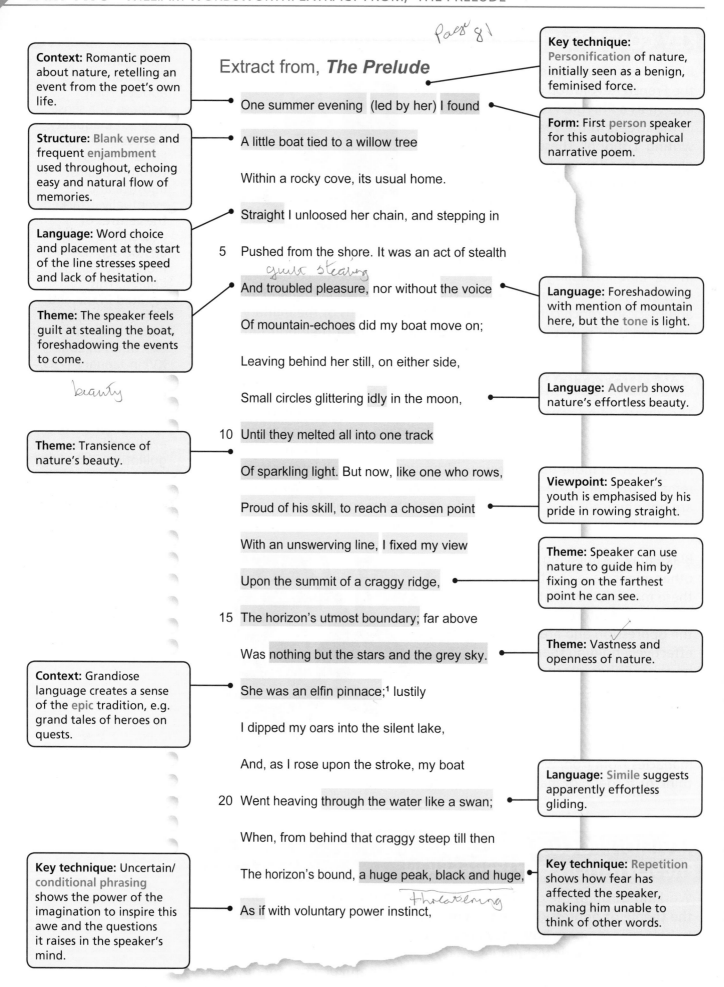

Poem 81

Extract from, *The Prelude*

Context: Romantic poem about nature, retelling an event from the poet's own life.

Key technique: Personification of nature, initially seen as a benign, feminised force.

One summer evening (led by her) I found

Form: First person speaker for this autobiographical narrative poem.

A little boat tied to a willow tree

Structure: Blank verse and frequent enjambment used throughout, echoing easy and natural flow of memories.

Within a rocky cove, its usual home.

Straight I unloosed her chain, and stepping in

Language: Word choice and placement at the start of the line stresses speed and lack of hesitation.

5   Pushed from the shore. It was an act of stealth

guilt stealing

And troubled pleasure, nor without the voice

Language: Foreshadowing with mention of mountain here, but the tone is light.

Theme: The speaker feels guilt at stealing the boat, foreshadowing the events to come.

Of mountain-echoes did my boat move on;

Leaving behind her still, on either side,

beauty

Small circles glittering idly in the moon,

Language: Adverb shows nature's effortless beauty.

Theme: Transience of nature's beauty.

10   Until they melted all into one track

Of sparkling light. But now, like one who rows,

Viewpoint: Speaker's youth is emphasised by his pride in rowing straight.

Proud of his skill, to reach a chosen point

With an unswerving line, I fixed my view

Theme: Speaker can use nature to guide him by fixing on the farthest point he can see.

Upon the summit of a craggy ridge,

15   The horizon's utmost boundary; far above

Was nothing but the stars and the grey sky.

Theme: Vastness and openness of nature. ✓

Context: Grandiose language creates a sense of the epic tradition, e.g. grand tales of heroes on quests.

She was an elfin pinnace;[1] lustily

I dipped my oars into the silent lake,

And, as I rose upon the stroke, my boat

Language: Simile suggests apparently effortless gliding.

20   Went heaving through the water like a swan;

When, from behind that craggy steep till then

Key technique: Uncertain/ conditional phrasing shows the power of the imagination to inspire this awe and the questions it raises in the speaker's mind.

The horizon's bound, a huge peak, black and huge,

threatening

As if with voluntary power instinct,

Key technique: Repetition shows how fear has affected the speaker, making him unable to think of other words.

Glossary
[1]   pinnace = a type of small boat

Key technique: Personification becomes more threatening and less humanised, lacking gender.

Theme: New malign representation of Nature separates the speaker from the stars, a source of light and comfort.

Key technique: Here again personification becomes more threatening and less humanised, lacking gender.

Voice: Shows how the speaker was affected initially.

Language: Nouns form a **semantic field** of depression to show the effect on the speaker.

Language: Return to key word used earlier shows enduring power of fear.

Upreared its head. I struck and struck again,

25 And growing still in stature the grim shape

Towered up between me and the stars, and still,

For so it seemed, with purpose of its own

And measured motion like a living thing,

Strode after me. With trembling oars I turned,

30 And through the silent water stole my way

Back to the covert of the willow tree;

returned home

There in her mooring-place I left my bark, –

And through the meadows homeward went, in grave

And serious mood; but after I had seen

35 That spectacle, for many days, my brain

Worked with a dim and undetermined sense

Of unknown modes of being; o'er my thoughts

There hung a darkness, call it solitude   *past experiences*

Or blank desertion. No familiar shapes

40 Remained, no pleasant images of trees,

Of sea or sky, no colours of green fields;

But huge and mighty forms, that do not live

Like living men, moved slowly through the mind

By day, and were a trouble to my dreams.

trouble

William Wordsworth (1770–1850)

Sound: Harsh consonant cluster/**alliteration** contributes to the frightening effect, **juxtaposing** the power of the mountain and the helplessness of the speaker.

Key technique: Uncertain phrasing emphasises imagined nature of the thing, linking to key Romantic theme of power of the Imagination.

Theme: Return to the comforting, homely side of nature; see the 'rocky cove' of line 3.

Language: Adjectives clearly create sense of fear and uncertainty.

Key technique: Repetition of negative phrases creates sense of experience haunting the speaker.

past

Theme: Power of imagination – the danger is in his mind. There is also the realisation of how powerless humans are in relation to nature and the world as a whole.

Wordsworth (1770–1850) is one of the best-known English Romantic poets and was Poet Laureate from 1843, although he refused at first, feeling that he was too old for the post. He grew up in Cumbria, spending most of his life there, and enjoyed considerable poetic success in his twenties. He is credited, together with his friend Samuel Taylor Coleridge, with starting the English Romantic movement.

'The Prelude' is Wordsworth's great autobiographical poem. It remained unfinished at the time of his death and was published in fourteen books. The extract in the cluster is from the first book, dealing with his childhood.

SUMMARY

- The speaker comes across a boat and uses it to row into a lake at night, noting the beauty of his surroundings.
- The boy is pleased with his skill in rowing and describes how he fixes his sight on a 'craggy ridge' (14) in the distance.
- A peak behind the ridge appears suddenly, seeming to chase the boy for stealing the boat.
- Frightened, the boy turns the boat around and returns it to its mooring.
- The speaker is haunted by the experience afterwards, unable to recall any pleasant details of his trip.

KEY ASPECTS OF THE POEM

A   Wordsworth uses a first person viewpoint to convey the story directly and to enable the reader to **empathise** with the speaker. Much of the speaker's language is **conversational**, for example the repeated connective 'and'.

B   Personification of nature is used throughout, from 'led by her' (1), which **refers** to the whole of nature as a **personified female**, to the 'huge peak' (22), which is **presented** as a threatening 'it'.

C   The poem is in the epic tradition, as it tells of an adventure, although it is an everyday story rather than a grand quest. In places, Wordsworth uses **fantastical language** that suits this form, such as 'elfin pinnace' (17) and 'upreared' (24).

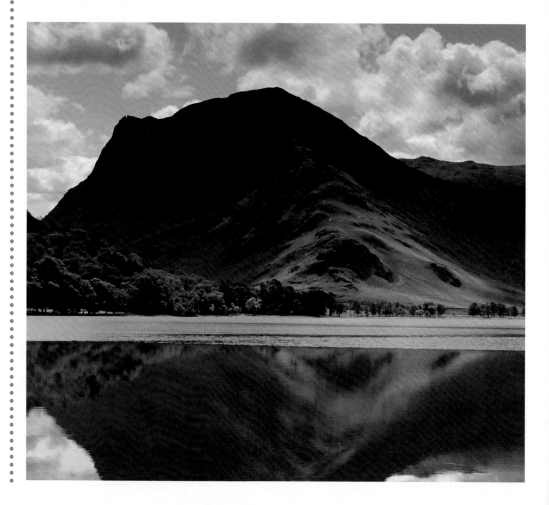

KEY SETTING: THE LAKE DISTRICT AT NIGHT (A01)

Wordsworth presents the reader with realistic descriptions of the lake and its surroundings at night, reflecting the Romantic movement's love of the natural world. Considerable attention is paid to the night sky, whether above the boat, or reflected in the water, which creates a sense of openness and isolation. This sense of space and the sheer size of the open water and sky enables Wordsworth to create a greater shock when the peak seems to rise up and the experience suddenly becomes threatening.

KEY TECHNIQUE: IMAGERY (A02)

Wordsworth makes considerable use of figurative language to show the power of nature in 'The Prelude'. He focuses the speaker's attention on small details to demonstrate the beauty in tiny things, such as 'Small circles glittering idly' (9). In this example, Wordsworth chooses the adverb 'idly' to emphasise how nature is beautiful in an effortless way. Later in the poem, the 'huge peak' (22) is personified to demonstrate the physical power of nature in a more forceful way, supported by the repetition of 'huge' and the speaker's frightened reaction.

> **CHECKPOINT 2** (A01)
>
> Which word in the first ten lines of the poem tells us that the boy is pleased with his cunning thievery?

> **TOP TIP** (A01)
>
> It is important to be able to identify how the poems in the cluster relate to ideas about power and conflict. Go through this poem and trace how Wordsworth sets up the conflict between the speaker and the darker side of nature.

EXAM FOCUS: WRITING ABOUT EFFECTS (A02)

You may be asked to write about how Wordsworth presents conflict in this poem. Read this example, which comments on the last part of the poem:

Clear statement linking technique to effect

Wordsworth uses repetition which shows how the speaker cannot stop thinking about what happened: 'No familiar shapes ... no pleasant images.' Through this repeated pattern, Wordsworth emphasises the negative burden weighing on the speaker after his trip – although we know he had a pleasant experience at the start of the boat trip, focusing on the beauty of small details, he cannot remember anything at all positive about it now.

Apt quotation

Shows the meaning of this section in the context of the whole poem

Now you try it:

Improve this paragraph by adding a concluding sentence or two to draw it together by referencing the idea of conflict explicitly.

Context: Set in sixteenth-century Italy and based on a real duchess who died in suspicious circumstances.

Viewpoint: Speaker is based on the Duke of Ferrara, Alfonso II d'Este.

Theme: The Duke mentions Frà Pandolf 'by design', i.e. deliberately, so that he can describe the Duchess's relationship with the man who painted her. The fact that Frà Pandolf was a monk suggests that the Duke's hints at impropriety are unlikely.

Language: Positioning of 'only' emphasises his belief that it should be only him who affects her in that way.

Language: Repetition highlights sense of excess.

Language: Exclamatory language, shows strength of his feelings.

Structure: Enjambment emphasises the word 'Broke', creating a violent and ominous effect.

My Last Duchess

Ferrara

That's my last Duchess painted on the wall,

Looking as if she were alive. I call

That piece a wonder, now: Frà Pandolf's hands

Worked busily a day, and there she stands.

5   Will't please you sit and look at her? I said

'Frà Pandolf' by design, for never read

Strangers like you that pictured countenance,

The depth and passion of its earnest glance,

But to myself they turned (since none puts by

10   The curtain I have drawn for you, but I)

And seemed as they would ask me, if they durst,

How such a glance came there; so, not the first

Are you to turn and ask thus. Sir, 'twas not

Her husband's presence **only**, called that spot

15   Of joy into the Duchess' cheek: perhaps

Frà Pandolf chanced to say 'Her mantle laps

Over my lady's wrist too much,' or 'Paint

Must never hope to reproduce the faint

Half-flush that dies along her throat': such stuff

20   Was courtesy, she thought, and cause enough

For calling up that spot of joy. She had

A heart – how shall I say? – too soon made glad,

Too easily impressed; she liked whate'er

She looked on, and her looks went everywhere.

25   Sir, 'twas all one! My favour at her breast,

The dropping of the daylight in the West,

The bough of cherries some officious fool

Broke in the orchard for her, the white mule

Structure: Rhyming couplets in iambic pentameter throughout show strict control of language, yet enjambment and caesurae create a natural conversational rhythm.

Form: Dramatic monologue – the Duke is addressing a specific audience (the representative of a count), rather than the reader.

Theme: The Duke is presented as controlling access even to the Duchess's image.

Theme: Meaning 'if they dared' – shows the Duke's sense of his own importance.

Structure: The Duchess's joyful reaction to compliments is juxtaposed with foreshadowing of her fate by the vocabulary, e.g. 'dies' and 'throat'.

Theme: The Duke saw his wife as not discerning enough, and free with her affections towards other men.

Theme: The Duke thinks it's obvious that his attention and wealth are worth more than the beauty of nature.

Language: Vocabulary emphasises universality of the Duchess's enthusiasm.

She rode with round the terrace – all and each

30 Would draw from her alike the approving speech,

Language: Longer caesurae and more broken-up lines here convey anger.

Or blush, at least. She thanked men, – good! but thanked

Somehow – I know not how – as if she ranked

Language: Verb shows importance of hierarchy.

Theme: Duke thought marrying her was giving her the history or heritage of his name and she should respect that.

My gift of a nine-hundred-years-old name

With anybody's gift. Who'd stoop to blame

Voice: Irony used by Browning as Duke clearly thinks he does have this skill.

35 This sort of trifling? Even had you skill

In speech – (which I have not) – to make your will

Language: Vocabulary highlights the Duke's view of the Duchess as an object.

Quite clear to such an one, and say, 'Just this

Or that in you disgusts me; here you miss,

Or there exceed the mark' – and if she let

Language: Verbs show the precision of the Duke's expectations.

Language: The verb shows the Duke's belief that it would be appropriate to teach or train his wife how to behave.

40 Herself be lessoned so, nor plainly set

Her wits to yours, forsooth, and made excuse,

– E'en then would be some stooping; and I choose

Theme: Shows the Duke's arrogance.

Never to stoop. Oh sir, she smiled, no doubt,

Whene'er I passed her; but who passed without

Language: Tone here is almost sarcastic, showing his anger.

Language: Ambiguity here – he implies he had her killed, but doesn't quite state it explicitly.

45 Much the same smile? This grew; I gave commands;

Then all smiles stopped together. There she stands

Language: Juxtaposition supports idea he had her killed and topic – shift back to the quality of the painting shows him as cold.

As if alive. Will't please you rise? We'll meet

Structure: Topic shifts from the Duchess here.

The company below, then. I repeat,

The Count your master's known munificence – *very generous*

Theme: Duke's arrogance and societal attitudes to women emphasised – purpose of conversation is to arrange another marriage.

50 Is ample warrant that no just pretence

Of mine for dowry will be disallowed;

Context: Some see this poem as critical of social norms regarding Victorian marriage, when dowries were still common.

Though his fair daughter's self, as I avowed

At starting, is my object. Nay, we'll go

Together down, sir. Notice Neptune, though,

Theme: The other art on display also has power and control as its theme.

55 Taming a sea-horse, thought a rarity,

Language: Closing on the first **person pronoun** emphasises his self-centredness and reflects the dramatic monologue form.

Theme: Social hierarchy is the poem's final note with the name-drop of this fictional artist, which again shows the Duke's pride in his possessions, as the person addressed in the monologue is clearly meant to know who this is.

Which Claus of Innsbruck cast in bronze for me!

Robert Browning (1812–1889)

KEY CONTEXT (A03)

Robert Browning (1812–89) was a lover of poetry and art from a young age. He visited Italy in 1838 for research and later returned there after marrying the poet Elizabeth Barrett. His marriage to Elizabeth was somewhat controversial, as she was older than him and her father was opposed to her marrying anyone. Many of Browning's monologues express criticisms of social norms, and these criticisms can also be seen in the way he chose to live.

SUMMARY

- The speaker, a duke, points out a portrait of his former wife, inviting the implied listener to admire its lifelike quality.
- The Duke implies that his wife may have been flirting with Frà Pandolf, the painter, and it quickly becomes clear that the Duke believed his wife was too friendly or flirtatious with everyone and did not appreciate her husband enough.
- The Duke expresses his belief that the power conferred upon his wife by marriage was highly valuable. He feels that she should have been grateful for this 'gift' (33). He also makes it clear that he did not feel able to explain this to her.
- The Duke hints that he had his wife killed and then discusses meeting the listener's master – a count – whose daughter the Duke hopes to marry.

KEY ASPECTS OF THE POEM

A The poem is a **dramatic monologue** that presents us with only the Duke's **voice** and point of view, and yet we are still able to discern that his version of events may be **unreliable**.

B Browning uses **iambic pentameter** in **rhyming couplets**, although he combines this with considerable **enjambment** and **caesurae** to create a **conversational rhythm** that feels informal.

C Browning presents the Duke as having no 'skill in speech' (35–6) and uses only a few examples of **imagery** to support this characterisation.

KEY SETTING: SIXTEENTH-CENTURY FERRARA (A03)

This poem is about the Duke of Ferrara, in northern Italy, whose first wife died at the age of seventeen in suspicious circumstances. At that time, and also in Browning's lifetime, women's sexuality was often regarded as dangerous. It was therefore controlled by society through arranged marriages which were likely to be based on family politics and to involve the payment of a dowry (a sum of money or property) by the bride's family to the husband.

KEY THEME: SOCIAL STATUS   **A02**

Browning makes it clear that the Duke is upset not just about the Duchess's perceived infidelity; he is also offended by the fact that she seems as content with less materially valuable gifts than the ones his marriage to her has conferred. He accuses her of being 'Too easily impressed' (23), which shows that he feels she should be more discerning. Browning depicts the Duke's irritation at his wife's enjoyment of nature, for example the sunset or a 'bough of cherries' (27), and even her happiness with a 'mule' (28), a lowly creature – not even a horse – to underscore his theme of social status and breeding. In the lines following the

references to these gifts (31–2), Browning uses longer caesurae to break up the lines, making the Duke's speech less fluent and representing his anger and loss of self-control.

CHECKPOINT 3   **A01**

The Duke has a statue of Neptune which he points out at the end of the poem, 'taming a sea-horse' (55). Who is Neptune?

KEY QUOTATION: THE POWER OF HIS NAME   **A02**

Browning shows the Duke's obsession with the value of his family name and history in the extended description 'My gift of a nine-hundred-years-old name' (33), which is made more important by use of the hyphenated **adjective** phrase to emphasise the age of the name. This gives the impression that the longevity of his family line is the most important gift that the Duchess could be given and perhaps implies that he is untouchable because of it. Further, the **verb** 'ranked' (32) emphasises the association with status and hierarchy. Instead of using a verb like 'valued' or 'prized' which has less to do with structure or hierarchy, Browning chooses this specific word with its connotations of grading and levels of worth.

AIMING HIGH: EXPLORING FORM   ⭐

Here Browning writes in the dramatic monologue form, but other poets in the cluster also use a single speaker in their poems. To achieve the highest grades you will need to explore how the dramatic monologue form differs from simply writing in a single voice, and to think about what makes this poem 'dramatic' and what effect that lends it. For example, the dramatic monologue form lends the poem an immediacy that makes it read like a live action scene, and provides the reader with a deliberately narrow perspective. Browning gradually unfolds a story from which we begin to infer that the Duke's jealousy and displeasure led to his wife's death, although the precise details are left unclear. Further drama also comes from the suggestion that perhaps another hapless woman may share the same fate. How do you think this compares with other poems in the cluster?   *power / victim*

Robert Browning

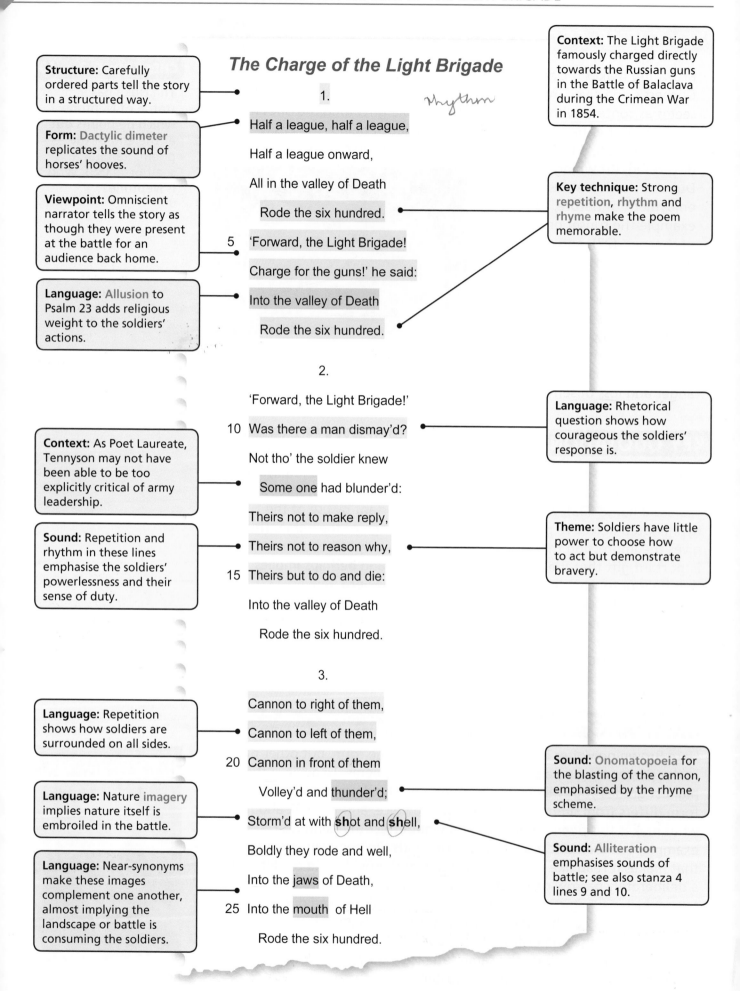

Context: The Light Brigade famously charged directly towards the Russian guns in the Battle of Balaclava during the Crimean War in 1854.

The Charge of the Light Brigade

Structure: Carefully ordered parts tell the story in a structured way.

Form: Dactylic dimeter replicates the sound of horses' hooves.

Viewpoint: Omniscient narrator tells the story as though they were present at the battle for an audience back home.

Language: Allusion to Psalm 23 adds religious weight to the soldiers' actions.

1.

Half a league, half a league,

Half a league onward,

All in the valley of Death

   Rode the six hundred.

5 'Forward, the Light Brigade!

Charge for the guns!' he said:

Into the valley of Death

   Rode the six hundred.

rhythm

Key technique: Strong repetition, rhythm and rhyme make the poem memorable.

2.

'Forward, the Light Brigade!'

10 Was there a man dismay'd?

Not tho' the soldier knew

   Some one had blunder'd:

Theirs not to make reply,

Theirs not to reason why,

15 Theirs but to do and die:

Into the valley of Death

   Rode the six hundred.

Context: As Poet Laureate, Tennyson may not have been able to be too explicitly critical of army leadership.

Sound: Repetition and rhythm in these lines emphasise the soldiers' powerlessness and their sense of duty.

Language: Rhetorical question shows how courageous the soldiers' response is.

Theme: Soldiers have little power to choose how to act but demonstrate bravery.

3.

Cannon to right of them,

Cannon to left of them,

20 Cannon in front of them

   Volley'd and thunder'd;

Storm'd at with shot and shell,

Boldly they rode and well,

Into the jaws of Death,

25 Into the mouth of Hell

   Rode the six hundred.

Language: Repetition shows how soldiers are surrounded on all sides.

Language: Nature imagery implies nature itself is embroiled in the battle.

Language: Near-synonyms make these images complement one another, almost implying the landscape or battle is consuming the soldiers.

Sound: Onomatopoeia for the blasting of the cannon, emphasised by the rhyme scheme.

Sound: Alliteration emphasises sounds of battle; see also stanza 4 lines 9 and 10.

4.

Language: Imagery of sight as well as sound.

Flash'd all their sabres bare,

Flash'd as they turn'd in air,

Language: Violent **verbs** highlight soldiers' actions, showing their bravery in battle.

Sabring the gunners there,

30 Charging an army, while

All the world wonder'd:

Plunged in the battery-smoke

Right thro' the line they broke;

Cossack and Russian

Theme: Propaganda – Tennyson describes the enemy under attack to show the success/bravery of the Light Brigade, while sanitising their suffering (see line 44, 'fell').

35 Reel'd from the sabre-stroke

Shatter'd and sunder'd. *split apart.*

Language: Repetition of single word creates a pause and slows the pace for this news.

Then they rode back, but not

Not the six hundred.

5.

Structure: Parallels to stanza 3 show the soldiers' return.

Cannon to right of them,

40 Cannon to left of them,

Cannon behind them

Volley'd and thunder'd;

Language: Vocabulary **choices** and alliteration create sense of sympathy.

Storm'd at with shot and shell,

While horse and hero fell,

Language: Altered prepositions from stanza 3 allow a mirrored structure but also show a deeper connection to the 'jaws of Death' and 'mouth of Hell' than before.

45 They that had fought so well

Came thro' the jaws of Death

Back from the mouth of Hell,

Language: Repetition emphasises the possible dual meaning here – what is left of individuals, as well as numerically left from the total.

All that was left of them,

Left of six hundred.

6.

Structure: Repetition of this line directs the reader's response to the soldiers – they deserve to be wondered at.

50 When can their glory fade?

O the wild charge they made!

All the world wonder'd.

Language: Imperative directs the audience's response to the Light Brigade.

Honour the charge they made!

Honour the Light Brigade,

Language: The only **adjective** attached to this repeated phrase in all six stanzas. It acts as an epithet to indicate how we should see them.

55 Noble six hundred!

Alfred Lord Tennyson (1809–1892)

KEY CONTEXT **A03**

Alfred Lord Tennyson (1809–92) was born and grew up in Lincolnshire. He attended Cambridge University but left before completing his degree, because his father died and he returned home to take care of his family. He was successful as a poet throughout his life and became Poet Laureate after Wordsworth's death in 1850.

SUMMARY

- Six hundred soldiers – the Light Brigade – charge forward, directly towards the Russian guns and into a valley, to engage in a battle between British and Russian troops during the Crimean War.
- In the valley they meet the enemy and are badly disadvantaged, but the soldiers press on bravely, not acknowledging that their leaders have made an error in sending them into this situation.
- The sounds and sights of battle are described, along with the few soldiers who return alive.
- The poem closes with a call to celebrate the bravery of the soldiers.

KEY ASPECTS OF THE POEM

A Tennyson uses a strong **rhythm** to replicate sounds like horses' hoofbeats and cannons.

B **Repetition** and **rhyme** combine to make the poem highly memorable.

C The poem's **structure** carefully presents the battle as a story in six stanzas, with **longer stanzas** for the battle itself and a short **concluding stanza** in which Tennyson makes clear how the reader should respond.

D Tennyson chooses many active **verbs** to create a very lively poem.

E Tennyson uses **onomatopoeia** in the deep 'un' of 'thunder'd' (21), which echoes cannon fire and is repeated through rhymes such as 'hundred' (17) and 'blunder'd' (12).

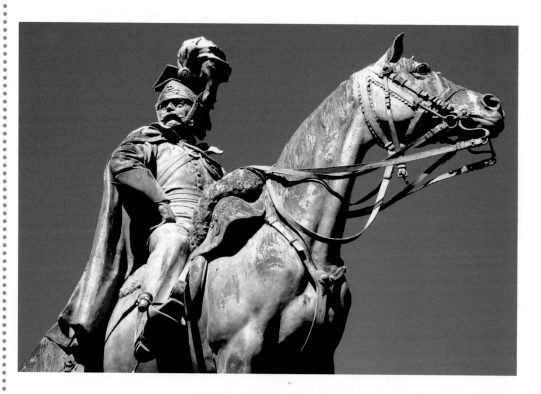

KEY SETTING: BATTLE OF BALACLAVA (A03)

Tennyson's poem is set in the famous (to his contemporary Victorian reader) Battle of Balaclava (1854), between British and Russian troops, in which the Light Brigade were reduced from well over 600 men to 195, partially because of a miscommunication of orders.

At the time of writing this poem, Tennyson was Poet Laureate, which meant that it was his responsibility to record national events in verse. This is perhaps why the attitude to the event is ambiguous in the poem. Victorian Britain was aware from news reports that 'Some one had blunder'd' (12) so it was not necessary for Tennyson to do more than mention this to bring it to the reader's mind. The idea is emphasised by being part of the rhyme with 'hundred', but the main thrust of the poem remains the glorification of the ordinary soldier's devotion to duty – a suitable theme for an official Laureate poem. At the same time, it is possible that Tennyson was using his position to question – as far as he was able – the morality of sending men into 'the jaws of Death' (46).

KEY TECHNIQUE: USE OF FORM (A02)

This is a poem which is well known particularly for its formal elements. The strong **dactylic dimeter** (one stressed syllable followed by two unstressed syllables, repeated twice per line) is used for most lines and helps to create a sense of booming cannon or cantering horses. The stanza patterns are also tightly controlled: each stanza finishes with the phrase 'six hundred' and all stanzas include rhymes or near rhymes with 'hundred' in shorter, indented lines which finish off earlier ideas. The formal strength of the poem echoes the nobility it claims for its subject matter of the 'six hundred'.

> **CHECKPOINT 4** (A02)
>
> Why does Tennyson repeat words such as 'hundred', 'thunder'd' and 'blunder'd'?

> **KEY CONTEXT** (A03)
>
> 'The valley of Death' (6) is a clear reference to the biblical Psalm 23, in which King David declares that he will not be afraid even in 'the valley of the shadow of death' because of his faith in God. Tennyson's Victorian readers would all have been familiar with this **allusion**.

REVISION FOCUS: WAR

Create a mind map of the different ways that the poems focusing on war in the cluster present this theme. You should include how the writers use techniques relating to structure, sound, **imagery** and **vocabulary**. To challenge yourself, note how each writer uses these techniques to present different attitudes to war.

Exposure

Viewpoint: Written as all the soldiers, showing it isn't just one individual's opinion or experience.

Sound: Sibilance creates a hissing effect (also see line 4).

Our brains ache, in the merciless iced east winds that knive

Key technique: Present **tense** creates immediacy and contributes to the sense of it all never ending.

us …

onomat

Wearied we keep awake because the night is silent …

most. NB

Language: Ellipses convey idea of endless emptiness.

Language: Metaphor for the soldiers themselves.

Low, drooping flares confuse our memory of the salient …

5   Worried by silence, sentries whisper, curious, nervous,

Sound: Many **rhymes** are part-rhymes, evoking tension, as the poem is disharmonious.

But nothing happens.

Key technique: Refrain-like **repetition** emphasises the monotony the soldiers are living through – it is used again as the final line.

onomatopoeia

Watching, we hear the mad gusts tugging on the wire,

onomatop

Like twitching agonies of men among its brambles.

Context: Barbed wire strung between the two sides in the area known as No Man's Land.

neverending ono.   ono

Northward, incessantly, the flickering gunnery rumbles,

Language: Vocabulary presents the actual fighting as unreal and something the soldiers can barely believe in any more.

10   Far off, like a dull rumour of some other war.

What are we doing here?

Theme: The presentation of war seems unreal, as the soldiers are so entrenched in their immediate physical suffering and unable to connect to anything else.

Language: Rhetorical question used to convey uncertainty and lack of conviction about why the soldiers are at war.

sad feeling

The poignant misery of dawn begins to grow …

Language: Tripartite list makes weather potentially more of a threat than war.

We only know war lasts, rain soaks, and clouds sag stormy.

sadness

Dawn massing in the east her melancholy army

Theme: Dawn, usually beautiful and benign in literature, is here seen as an enemy.

15   Attacks once more in ranks on shivering ranks of grey,

Key technique: Personification of the weather, compares it to the beleaguered army.

But nothing happens.

ono   onom.

Language: Connective emphasises that this is contrary to expectations.

Sudden successive flights of bullets streak the silence.

Sound: Sibilance makes bullets sound soft, reducing their threat.

Theme: The environment and weather seem more of a threat than the war at this point.

Less deadly than the air that shudders black with snow,

allit

With sidelong flowing flakes that flock, pause, and renew,

Sound: Alliteration with the consonant cluster is discordant and disruptive to the line; the opposite of 'flowing'.

20   We watch them wandering up and down the wind's

Language: Personification presents the wind as indifferent and detached.

nonchalance, *indifferent / uncaring*

But nothing happens.

Language: Snow is personified in a sinister way, highlighting its invasive and personal attack.

Context: References to the trenches they were fighting in and from.

Structure: Movement of time from winter to spring/thaw but no change in the soldiers' experience.

Sound: Assonance emphasises the sluggishness of movement – even their imaginations can't get them home quickly.

Theme: Nature has taken over their homes as well as attacking them on the battlefield.

Language: Vocabulary presents God as powerful rather than benevolent.

Theme: Soldiers have lost all hope and accept what they see as their fate.

Sound: Short vowel sounds create a pinching, shrivelled-up tone as the soldiers are dehumanised by being presented in pieces rather than as whole human beings.

Form: Use of near-rhyme, a refrain-like repetition, hissing sibilance and discordant alliteration echo the themes of misery and fear of dying from exposure.

Pale flakes with fingering stealth come feeling for our faces –

We cringe in holes, back on forgotten dreams, and stare,

    snow-dazed,

25 Deep into grassier ditches. So we drowse, sun-dozed,

Littered with blossoms trickling where the blackbird fusses.

     – Is it that we are dying?

Slowly our ghosts drag home: glimpsing the sunk fires, glozed

30 With crusted dark-red jewels; crickets jingle there;
    fun

For hours the innocent mice rejoice: the house is theirs;

Shutters and doors, all closed: on us the doors are closed, –

    We turn back to our dying.

Since we believe not otherwise can kind fires burn;

35 Nor ever suns smile true on child, or field, or fruit.

For God's invincible spring our love is made afraid;
    Powerful

Therefore, not loath, we lie out here; therefore were born,
    hate

    For love of God seems dying.

Tonight, His frost will fasten on this mud and us,
    God's

40 Shrivelling many hands, puckering foreheads crisp.

The burying-party, picks and shovels in shaking grasp,

Pause over half-known faces. All their eyes are ice,

    But nothing happens.

Wilfred Owen (1893–1918)

Language: Unusual compound phrases (showing how the soldiers are exposed to the elements) reflect the soldiers' sense of unreality/confusion.

Language: Repetition reinforces the impossibility of returning home, even in their imagination.

Language: Tripartite list emphasises life through symbols of fertility and growth, which seems to mock the soldiers.

Language: Passive construction emphasises effect on soldiers' emotions.

Theme: Soldiers have become part of the landscape along with the 'mud'.

Language: Metaphor conveys the loss of emotion in the soldiers' frozen, death-like state.

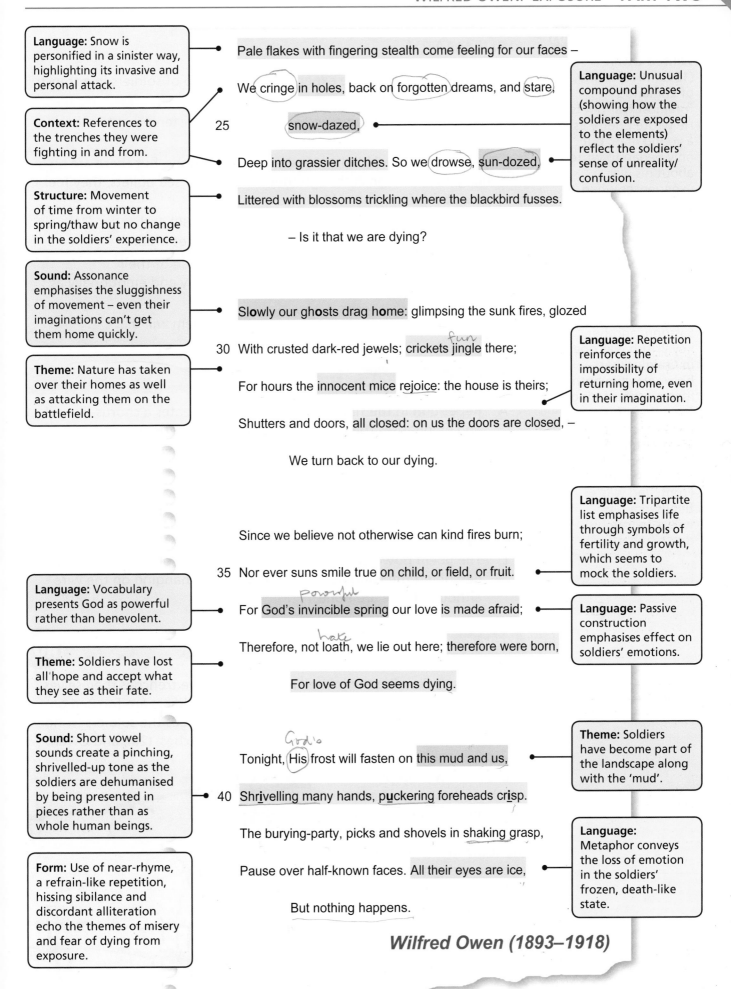

KEY CONTEXT (A03)

Wilfred Owen (1893–1918) is one of England's foremost war poets. He wrote poetry as a young man, but only began to write about his war experiences when suffering from shell shock (which we would now call post-traumatic stress disorder) in 1917, under the guidance of Siegfried Sassoon. Owen met Sassoon, another key British war poet, in Craiglockhart hospital while both men were suffering from the effects of the war. This poem was written in 1918, after Owen had returned to the Front, and was finalised a few weeks before his death in battle.

SUMMARY

- The poem describes the experiences of a group of soldiers in a trench in the First World War.
- The soldiers are freezing and exhausted from listening out in the silence.
- They feel attacked by the weather and conditions, but there are no changes in the war. Although they occasionally see bullets, they feel more at risk from the cold.
- They think about home, about how 'crickets' (30) and 'mice' (31) are indoors and warm while they are not able to get inside.
- The soldiers are losing their faith in God because of their predicament; they are out in the cold spiritually and emotionally as well as literally.
- Frost settles on them at night, and some of them will die.

KEY ASPECTS OF THE POEM

- **A**   Repetition in the final line of each stanza creates a **chorus-like effect** and emphasises the soldiers' monotonous experience.
- **B**   The viewpoint Owen chooses clearly shows the soldiers as a united group through use of the pronouns **we/us/our**. This is further supported by the **present tense**, which gives the poem immediacy.
- **C**   The considerable use of half-rhyme has an **unsettling effect**.
- **D**   Owen uses alliteration of soft sounds – particularly sibilance – to support the impression of near-silence and whispering.
- **E**   The poem **powerfully evokes** the images and sounds of war, e.g. describing the wind by calling to mind men hanging on the wire although there are none.

KEY SETTING: THE TRENCHES   (A01)

Owen doesn't describe the immediate setting of the trenches themselves, but their wider surroundings, as that is what the soldiers are focused on as they wait for something to happen. The reader sees the soldiers 'cringe in holes' (24) which are compared with 'grassier ditches' (26), and Owen refers to 'the wire' (6) of No Man's Land, a concept with which readers would have been familiar. The poem as a whole is not about setting the scene of the trenches, but about evoking the experience, so Owen's description focuses on sound and sensation from outside the trench.

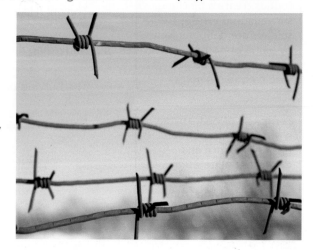

KEY TECHNIQUE: PRESENT TENSE **A02**

Owen's use of the present tense throughout this poem has the effect of creating immediacy for the reader: whenever you read the poem, it appears to be happening 'now'. At the same time, and more important, the tense makes the soldiers' experiences seem never-ending. When we read 'we keep awake because the night is silent' (3), there is no sense of 'until' something else happens – we are just given the non-conclusion 'But nothing happens' (6), making clear that this impossible state of exposure continues without resolution.

TOP TIP: WRITING ABOUT SOUND **A02**

Notice how Owen uses sibilance and other alliteration in stanza four. Its opening line recreates the sound of bullets in the air with 'sudden successive ... streak the silence' (17). The softness of this sound reinforces Owen's claim that the bullets are 'less deadly than the air' (18), while he interrupts the flow of the stanza, just as the snow interrupts the air, with the more jarring alliteration of 'flowing flakes that flock' (19).

The next line also uses alliteration – on 'w' this time – to emphasise the random nature of the flakes and the wind's 'nonchalance' (21), which we could contrast with the dawn's aggression in stanza three. The wind is also **personified** and may be harming the soldiers, but it is doing so haphazardly, rather than in the militaristic and deliberate way that the dawn 'attacks' in lines 12–15. Note how each of these examples of alliteration has a different effect and ensure you can comment on these specifically.

KEY QUOTATION: THE SOLDIERS' POWERLESSNESS **A02**

Owen focuses on the soldiers' readiness for action and the repeated dashing of their expectations with the paradoxical phrase 'But nothing happens' (6). The connective 'but' demonstrates that 'nothing' is not what is expected to happen, and Owen repeats this phrase to highlight that this state of unfulfilled tension is the soldiers' continuous experience, over and over again. This idea is a paradox, but it is the case that it is nothing that is killing the soldiers. The effect of this repetition on the reader is wearying, allowing us to extend sympathy to the soldiers in their predicament.

CHECKPOINT 5 **A02**

'Dawn massing in the east her melancholy army' (14) is an example of which literary feature?

Context: The Northern Ireland Assembly's parliament buildings are commonly known as Stormont; this poem can be read as political allegory.

Poem with hidden meaning

Context: This poem was written at the start of 'the Troubles' in Ireland and may therefore refer to outbreaks of disorder/violence in the early days.

Storm on the Island

Viewpoint: Whole community.

Language: Present tense creates immediacy.

We are prepared: we build our houses squat,

Form: Blank verse with irregular enjambment and caesurae mimics natural speech.

Language: Verb used with ironic tone to imply hay would end up being a problem, if it was able to grow.

Sink walls in rock and roof them with good slate.

Wrinkled with age

This wizened earth has never troubled us

With hay, so, as you see, there are no stacks

Key technique: Nature personified as potentially seeming friendly.

5 Or stooks that can be lost. Nor are there trees

Language: Colloquial/conversational.

friendly

Which might prove company when it blows full

Key technique: Personification develops a sense of danger/warning – in classical drama 'choruses' commented on the action to ensure the audience understood the implications.

Language: Blast of the wind emphasised through structure (enjambment) and sound (alliteration).

orbit

Blast: you know what I mean – leaves and branches

danger / warning

Can raise a tragic chorus in a gale

noise

So that you can listen to the thing you fear

Theme: We can become seduced by drama, forgetting how dangerous it is; alternatively, this distraction would be comforting – but it is not available, stressing the hard, barren landscape.

10 Forgetting that it pummels your house too.

But there are no trees, no natural shelter.

Language: Pronoun seems to create an advisory tone.

You might think that the sea is company, — *nature being safe?*

Language: Repetition of key words from earlier reinforces key idea of nature seeming safe.

Exploding comfortably down on the cliffs

Language: Definite expression through precise connective and present tense presents storm as certainty, not just possibility.

But no: when it begins, the flung spray hits

15 The very windows, spits like a tame cat

Language: Simile evokes sense of something once trusted becoming unpredictable and violent.

unpredictable

Turned savage. We just sit tight while wind dives

bombs/gunfire   *(many guns shooting)*

Language: Militaristic semantic field once the storm is at full force.

And strafes invisibly. Space is a salvo,

We are bombarded by the empty air.

Theme: Wind, which does a lot of harm, is not an actual thing – what implications might this have allegorically or symbolically?

Language: Reference to the blasting effect of bombs, which create a vacuum.

Strange, it is a huge nothing that we fear.

Seamus Heaney (1939–2013)

SUMMARY

- The speaker explains how the community's houses are well equipped to last through storms, built of strong materials and low to the ground.
- The land is not the type to grow hay or trees, which can be difficult in high winds, but that means the landscape is wide open.
- The speaker also discusses the sea's behaviour in a storm – the cliffs do not protect the people, and spray can still reach them.
- The speaker compares the wind and the very air to gunfire and concludes that it is the air itself that frightens people in a storm: 'a huge nothing' (19).

KEY ASPECTS OF THE POEM

A   Heaney uses the plural pronoun 'we' (1) to create a viewpoint which is that of the whole community.

B   There are several examples of personification, similes and metaphors which Heaney uses to **imply intention or emotion** on the part of nature and the weather.

C   Heaney creates a **conversational** tone using informal direct address and colloquial phrases in blank verse.

D   There is a semantic field relating to attack which **increases in strength** through the poem. Group of words belonging to same category.

E   The poem's violent imagery hints at Ireland's troubled past.

KEY CONTEXT A03

Seamus Heaney (1939–2013) is one of Northern Ireland's best-known and best-loved poets. He taught poetry in both Harvard and Oxford universities and was awarded the Nobel Prize for Literature. In 2009, the year of his seventieth birthday, it was announced that two-thirds of the poetry books sold in the UK that year were his. His poetry is known for its rich, sensory quality and for focusing on topics that many people can relate to, such as family and the landscape.

Wrinkled with age

KEY SETTING: EXPOSED COTTAGES ON IRELAND'S COAST   A02

Heaney conjures up the setting of these 'squat' (1) houses for the reader with a wealth of description and **imagery**. Notice how he **personifies** and ascribes intentions to the landscape and weather throughout the poem. This begins with 'This wizened earth has never troubled us / With hay' (3–4), where the **adjective** 'wizened' suggests old age and is usually only applied to people, while the **verb** 'troubled' implies that the lack of crops is a blessing in disguise, as hay would only be lost in the storms anyway.

This sense of the landscape as potential 'company' (6) continues with the **simile** 'spits like a tame cat / Turned savage' (15–16), which perfectly captures the sea's spray hitting the cottage's windows, but makes this a spiteful and possibly dangerous act, as a 'savage' cat carries connotations of unpredictability. Finally, Heaney presents the sky itself as aggressive with vocabulary from a militaristic **semantic field**: 'dives', 'strafes', 'salvo', 'bombarded' (16–18). *like war*

KEY TECHNIQUE: TONE   A02

The poem is written in **blank verse** and in the present **tense**, both of which feel approachable and conversational. Heaney creates a chatty and sometimes humorous or ironic **tone** by addressing the audience directly using **colloquial** phrases, for example, 'as you see' (4), 'you know what I mean' (7). The poem as a whole therefore feels as if the speaker is thinking aloud, and it seems as though the final line catches the speaker by surprise or has just occurred to them.

P14   The Prelude (the power of nature)

CHECKPOINT 6   A02

What kind of words are 'tragic', 'flung' and 'savage' as used in lines 8, 14 and 16?

★ AIMING HIGH: WRITING ABOUT IMAGERY

An excellent way to show higher levels of understanding and analysis is to look for patterns. Although it is useful to analyse a single simile or **metaphor**, it is equally worthwhile to give an overview of how a writer creates an overall picture using imagery. For example, Heaney begins a pattern by presenting a natural element as possible 'company' (7), but then shows how it turns against the people, and how this escalates from the 'tragic chorus' of trees (8), through the sea's behaviour 'like a tame cat / Turned savage' (15–16) to the wind which acts like a wartime attack that 'dives / And strafes' (16–17).

Context: Clearly sets poem in First World War, although Hughes was not alive then.

Form: Three stanzas split the scene like three acts, but uneven rhythm and line lengths echo the soldier's haphazard progress.

Sound: Alliteration adds intensity to the discomfort of his physical experience.

Viewpoint: Third person presenting the soldier's experience from the outside.

Key technique: Sensory imagery creates sense of the soldier's physical experience.

Bayonet Charge

Suddenly he awoke and was running – raw

In raw-seamed hot khaki, his sweat heavy,

Stumbling across a field of clods towards a green hedge

That dazzled with rifle fire, hearing

5 Bullets smacking the belly out of the air –

He lugged a rifle numb as a smashed arm;

The patriotic tear that had brimmed in his eye

Sweating like molten iron from the centre of his chest, –

In bewilderment then he almost stopped –

10 In what cold clockwork of the stars and the nations

Was he the hand pointing that second? He was running

Like a man who has jumped up in the dark and runs

Listening between his footfalls for the reason

Of his still running, and his foot hung like

15 Statuary in mid-stride. Then the shot-slashed furrows

Threw up a yellow hare that rolled like a flame

And crawled in a threshing circle, its mouth wide

Open silent, its eyes standing out.

He plunged past with his bayonet toward the green hedge,

20 King, honour, human dignity, etcetera

Dropped like luxuries in a yelling alarm

To get out of that blue crackling air

His terror's touchy dynamite.

Ted Hughes (1930–1998)

Language: Unusual verb conveys soldier's difficulty seeing due to gunfire.

Key technique: Simile implies the rifle disables him or impairs his movements and emphasises the violence of war.

Language: Soldier suddenly questions what he's doing, reflected by abrupt line ending.

Key technique: Imagery creates distance and implies he sees himself from the outside or experiences events in a disconnected way.

Theme: The soldier is unaware of why he is doing what he is doing, or even why he is there.

Key technique: Simile shows soldier's absolute stillness but also implies beauty and that someone else – a sculptor – is in control.

Theme: Usual war poetry themes, concepts seen as worth fighting for – the structure is used to question this.

Key technique: Physical imagery evokes sounds of battle, but turns their effect on to the environment rather than people.

Key technique: Simile suggests heat and links his heart and the 'tear', implying a contrast between patriotism and harsh reality.

Language: Metaphor suggests soldier is part of the machinery of the universe, as if he doesn't have control.

Structure: Syntax echoes message with sentences ending abruptly and restarting, just as the ideas do.

Theme: Hare acts as a warning by jolting him out of his own panic and is a metaphor for the soldiers trapped in war.

Language: Repeated phrase from first stanza shows soldier is back on original course.

Language: Vocabulary choice at end of list devalues other items and shows that the soldier now has different priorities – mere survival.

Language: Alliteration implies that he could be destroyed by his own fear.

SUMMARY

- A soldier runs through rifle fire holding a rifle with bayonet attached.
- The soldier becomes confused and pauses for a split second, unsure what he is doing.
- The soldier notices a hare in the battlefield, which thrashes about, dying.
- The soldier stops thinking and resumes the charge.

KEY ASPECTS OF THE POEM

A   Hughes uses an erratic structure in terms of **rhythm** and line length to mirror the soldier's movements.

B   **Sound features** like **alliteration** and short vowels **evoke the chaos** of the battlefield.

C   Hughes uses a range of **powerful and evocative** imagery.

KEY SETTING: A FIRST WORLD WAR BATTLEFIELD

Hughes evokes the sights, sounds and sensations of the battlefield through the soldier's experience of it. This is a shocking experience that we, like the soldier, are plunged into with the opening 'Suddenly' (1), and this sense of confusion and disorientation is present throughout the poem. Details are described, but we are never given a picture of the whole setting – and this is deliberate, as part of the soldier's overwhelming bewilderment. Hughes also carefully uses structure in a way that mimics this confusion, with uneven line lengths, irregular punctuation and unfinished sentences contributing to this effect.

In the first stanza, Hughes describes 'a green hedge / That dazzled with rifle fire' as a kind of marker that the soldier is 'stumbling ... towards' (3–4). The **verb** 'dazzled' is an unusually positive-sounding choice, and depicts the hedge as lit up by the firing of the rifles, although it does convey something that is hard to look at and that perhaps reduces the soldier's vision. Then, in the final stanza, once the soldier has determined to continue charging, he plunges once more 'toward the green hedge' (19), so we can see that Hughes repeats the phrase to show the soldier's return to the same path.

KEY TECHNIQUE: IMAGERY (A02)

Hughes's use of imagery in this poem is varied and connects the battlefield to a range of more common, everyday ideas and objects, such as 'clockwork' (10), perhaps because he is writing for a 1950s audience and not one recently returned from the First World War. Hughes creates a very physical sense of the experience in the first stanza, with the **metaphors** of 'heavy' sweat (2) and bullets 'smacking the belly out of the air' (5), along with the **simile** 'a rifle numb as a smashed arm' (6). All of this bodily imagery focuses heavily on the physicality of the soldier, even though most of it is not actually about him. The effect is to reinforce the idea of him physically struggling to drag himself across the field, through the mud, to charge at the enemy.

KEY CONTEXT (A03)

As a country man, Hughes was familiar with the sight of hares running across fields. They are rarely seen except for a flash, and are intelligent creatures. A hare 'crawl[ing] in a threshing circle' (17) is a horrific symbol of the damage caused by war, and a key image of the poem. Images of First World War battlefields typically reveal how woods and fields were utterly destroyed.

KEY QUOTATION: ABANDONED IDEALS (A01)

The soldier's rapid shift from inaction into action is mirrored in the fast-paced listing 'King, honour, human dignity, etcetera / Dropped like luxuries in a yelling alarm / To get out of that blue crackling air' (20–2). Hughes presents us with a list of ideas usually associated with war, but quickly undermines their impact with the dismissive 'etcetera', before revealing that they are 'Dropped like luxuries' as the soldier's only motivation becomes self-preservation and not bravery or nobility.

EXAM FOCUS: WRITING ABOUT CONFLICTS (A02)

Writing about less obvious kinds of conflict is a good way to expand your answer. Read this example, which discusses the internal conflict that Hughes presents the soldier as experiencing:

Clear focus on writer's technique	Hughes uses a simile to show how the soldier's mental conflict affects him so completely that he freezes: 'his foot hung like / Statuary in mid-stride.' This shows how the soldier is completely still and seems almost lifeless, like a statue. It also emphasises the incompleteness of his movement, as he has not even finished his step.	*Clear statement about the effect of the simile*
Well-chosen and correctly presented quotation, embedded into the answer		*Unpicks the meaning and impact of the quotation*

Now you try it:

Write one or two sentences that develop the paragraph further by linking the point made at the end more concretely to the original idea about mental conflict.

Theme: The title reflects that both physical and psychological leftovers feature in the poem.

Context: Based on a genuine soldier's account of his experiences, as related to Armitage.

ordinary conversation

Language: Strongly colloquial throughout, showing the soldier's English voice in a foreign land to emphasise his displacement.

Voice: Starts mid-story; speaker is relating an event he and at least two others were involved in.

Remains

On another occasion, we get sent out
to tackle looters raiding a bank.
And one of them legs it up the road,
probably armed, possibly not.

5 Well myself and somebody else and somebody else
are all of the same mind,
so all three of us open fire.
Three of a kind all letting fly, and I swear

I see every round as it rips through his life –
10 I see broad daylight on the other side.
So we've hit this looter a dozen times
and he's there on the ground, sort of inside out,

pain itself, the image of agony.
One of my mates goes by
15 and tosses his guts back into his body.
Then he's carted off in the back of a lorry.

End of story, except not really.
His blood-shadow stays on the street, and out on patrol
I walk right over it week after week.
20 Then I'm home on leave. But I blink

and he bursts again through the doors of the bank.
Sleep, and he's probably armed, possibly not.
Dream, and he's torn apart by a dozen rounds.
And the drink and the drugs won't flush him out –

25 he's here in my head when I close my eyes,
dug in behind enemy lines,
not left for dead in some distant, sun-stunned, sand-smothered land
or six-feet-under in desert sand,

but near to the knuckle, here and now,
30 his bloody life in my bloody hands.

Page 68, 71

Simon Armitage (b. 1963)

Theme: Insistence on all three being involved doesn't make the speaker feel less responsible.

Language: Metaphorical usage reflects the impact it had on the soldier.

Language: Verbs imply desensitisation to violence and lack of respect for human life.

Key technique: Irony – it's anything but over.

Form: Irregular rhythm and pace of natural speech created by sentence structures.

Theme: The soldier is haunted by that one memory despite attempts at self-medicating; hints of PTSD (post-traumatic stress disorder).

Sound: Sibilance combined with other consonants makes this jarring and slow, like the soldier constantly tripping over this memory.

cover up the truth

Key technique: The everyday language is a euphemism for the man's intestines having been spilled by the gunfire – perhaps showing a reluctance by the speaker to face up to the reality.

suggestions

Language: Connotations of the shadow-like stain are dark and menacing – like a shadow of death that hangs over the soldier.

Structure: Enjambment echoes memory constantly repeating through soldier's mind – there is no break from it.

Theme: Tormenting power of a single moment.

Language: Idiom suggests it's hard to bear.

Language: 'bloody' used as a curse as well as literally shows the soldier's anger that he has to live with this, as well as revealing his clear sense of responsibility.

SUMMARY

- The speaker describes being sent to deal with looters (robbers taking advantage of the war) at a bank in a Middle Eastern war zone.
- One of the looters runs away and the speaker and two others open fire on him, hitting him with about twelve rounds, and spilling his internal organs onto the street.
- The speaker's friend puts the man's guts back inside and the body is taken away.
- The speaker recalls seeing the man's 'blood-shadow' (18) on the street when on patrol – i.e. the blood left by the body on the pavement. He goes on to describe being haunted by images of the looter long afterwards, implying a metaphorical shadow left by the man in the speaker's life, which turning to drink and drugs cannot erase.   *represents something else*

KEY ASPECTS OF THE POEM

A A strongly colloquial **voice** is used, with many **informal phrases**.

B Armitage uses repetition of ideas, phrased in different ways, to show how the speaker's mind keeps going over the events

C Armitage creates a symbolic afterlife for the victim in the poem, using an **internalised and more poetic voice** for the continuing impact of his death which contrasts with the anecdotal, **everyday recounting** of the initial event.   *short, entertaining story*

D Armitage chooses a title with various *refers to* connotations, including: the idea of **human remains**; the **persistent memories** the soldier has; **what is left** of the soldier after his experiences.

③

KEY CONTEXT   **A03**

Simon Armitage (b. 1963) was born in Huddersfield, studied Geography at Portsmouth Polytechnic and worked as a probation officer in Greater Manchester until 1994. His MA thesis focused on the effects of television violence on young offenders, and his poetry often reflects concern about how people are affected by violence around them. He has written and published in many forms, including for TV and radio, and prose as well as poetry.

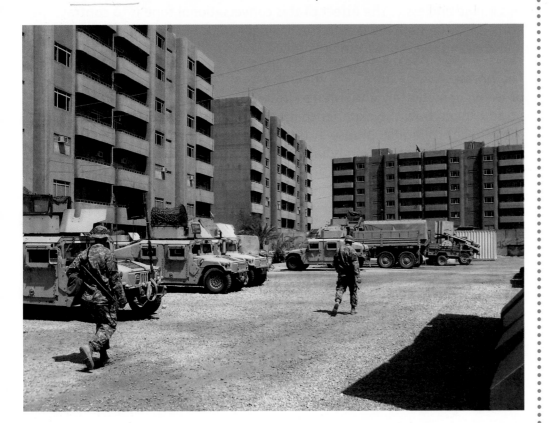

KEY CONTEXT (A03)

This poem comes from a collection of war poetry called *The Not Dead*, for which Armitage interviewed many soldiers. He then made a Channel 4 documentary about this collection, which includes footage of the soldier talking about the incident on which this poem is based. Make sure you consider how the subject matter of 'Remains' links to the title of Armitage's collection.

KEY SETTING: MIDDLE EASTERN WAR ZONE (A02)

Armitage keeps the precise setting vague. At first, we encounter a **semantic field** of only urban references: 'bank' (2), 'road' (3), 'lorry' (16), 'street' (18). The real detail comes at the end, once the speaker is at home and unable to forget the man he helped kill. Here Armitage provides a list of **adjectives** – 'distant, sun-stunned, sand-smothered' (27) – to convey the speaker's impression of the country he was in. The two hyphenated adjectives show the speaker's sympathy with a land which he views as being at the mercy of the elements. They are preceded by 'some', which helps show the soldier's negative attitude to that country, due to his disturbing experiences there, and emphasises the relative unimportance of the precise location: it is what has happened to the soldier on a personal level which matters, not the particular conflict and specific setting.

KEY TECHNIQUE: CONVERSATIONAL TONE (A02)

ordinary conversation

Armitage's chatty style creates a strongly personal **voice** for the soldier, by using many informal words and colloquial phrases. It is easy to imagine that this poem is part of a conversation, with a soldier telling his experiences to a group of friends. The opening feels like the middle of a story, with 'another occasion' (1) implying that **anecdotes** have already been exchanged. The **tone** is then firmly set with the **colloquialism** 'legs it' (3). Unnecessary **repetitions** like 'myself and somebody else and somebody else' (5) mimic the uncertainties of spontaneous speech, while also creating anonymity for the soldiers in the poem. Armitage uses speech features such as **discourse markers** as in the 'So' of 'So we've hit this looter a dozen times' (11), again both creating the impression of speech and allowing Armitage to repeat the idea of the man being shot multiple times, just as the soldier's mind replays this image endlessly. The effect of this conversational tone is to contrast the horror of what happened with the ordinary voice of the soldier recounting it, increasing the shock to the reader.

The phrase 'End of story' (17), meaning 'that was that', is a strong example of **irony**, immediately undermined in the poem itself as the speaker goes on to explain how the experience is anything but over. Here Armitage uses the familiar colloquial phrase at the opening of the stanza perhaps as a kind of bravado which immediately falls apart, showing how the conflict experience has affected this soldier.

REVISION FOCUS: STRONG VOICES

Using 'Remains' and two other poems which you think are effective in terms of how they create a voice, draw up a three-column table to record:

● What you think is **effective** about the voice in the poem

● A **quotation** that shows this

● Some **focused analysis** of your chosen quotation

Page 68, 71, 75, 79, 82, 84, 88   *Page 7*

Form: Stanzas in two different lengths + lines of around 10 syllables = control without rigidity, creating sense of natural speech.

Context: Sunday closest to Armistice Day (11 November), the anniversary of the truce that ended the First World War.

Language: Complex past **tense** prepares us for complex timelines.

Poppies

Language: Language of pain/imagery of bloody wounds perhaps foreshadowing events or reflecting her fears.

Viewpoint: A mother whose son is at war; these are her memories.

Three days before Armistice Sunday
and poppies had already been placed
on individual war graves. Before you left,
I pinned one onto your lapel, crimped petals,
5 spasms of paper red, disrupting a blockade
of yellow bias binding around your blazer.

Language: Language from a military semantic field. Words related in same category *(handwritten: P83)*

Language: **Connotations** of injury or protecting herself like a boxer.

Theme: Lots of detail of his clothing, maybe implies it was too difficult to focus on his face.

Sellotape bandaged around my hand,
I rounded up as many white cat hairs
as I could, smoothed down your shirt's
10 upturned collar, steeled the softening
of my face. I wanted to graze my nose
across the tip of your nose, play at
being Eskimos like we did when
you were little. I resisted the impulse
15 to run my fingers through the gelled
blackthorns of your hair. All my words
flattened, rolled, turned into felt,

Theme: Memories of the son's childhood come back to the mother as she prepares to send him off to war.

Form: **Enjambment** supports idea of words joining together in melting.

Language: **Simile** implies possibilities, yet he's heading off to war.

Key technique: Strong contrast to all the fabric imagery, conveying the strength she wanted to show.

Context: Weir is also a textile artist and this is reflected in her chosen imagery.

slowly melting. I was brave, as I walked
with you, to the front door, threw
20 it open, the world overflowing
like a treasure chest. A split second
and you were away, intoxicated.
After you'd gone I went into your bedroom,
released a song bird from its cage.
25 Later a single dove flew from the pear tree,
and this is where it has led me,
skirting the church yard walls, my stomach busy
making tucks, darts, pleats, hat-less, without
a winter coat or reinforcements of scarf, gloves.

Language: **Metaphor** for the mother's crying.

Key technique: Metaphor conveys uncertainty/concern through clothing-related imagery.

Key technique: Ambiguity, as some assume her son's name is there, or she may be connecting with others through history.

Language: Time markers used throughout poem to manage complex time shifts.

Key technique: Ambiguity in the symbolism: peace and perhaps freedom through death.

See 'blockade' in line 5.

30 On reaching the top of the hill I traced
the inscriptions on the war memorial,
leaned against it like a wishbone.
The dove pulled freely against the sky,
an ornamental stitch. I listened, hoping to hear
35 your playground voice catching on the wind.

Key technique: Metaphor combines both bird and textiles imagery, pulling together the mother's feelings of tension and longing for peace.

Jane Weir (b. 1963)

Theme: Implies comfort in a return to old patterns of behaviour.

Language: Simile implies she's making a wish as well as perhaps linking to family mealtime memories.

KEY CONTEXT (A03)

Jane Weir (b. 1963) is an Anglo-Italian poet and textile designer. This poem was written to fulfil a commission in 2009 from Carol Ann Duffy, who was seeking poems on the topic of war in response to the Gulf Wars and the Iraq inquiry.

SUMMARY

- The speaker describes seeing poppies on graves before Armistice Day.
- The speaker, a mother, remembers pinning a poppy to her son's blazer.
- She describes the differences between how she wanted to act and how she did act when he left for war.
- After the son left, the mother went upstairs to his bedroom and she refers to releasing a bird from its cage.
- She goes to the churchyard, without winter clothes, and visits the war memorial, hoping to hear her son's voice from the playground as she did when he was still at school.

KEY ASPECTS OF THE POEM

A The poem uses the first person and direct address, showing the voice of the mother speaking to the son.

B Weir uses connectives to create a **time frame** for the poem centred on the son's departure, as though everything is measured in relation to that event.

C There is a strong semantic field relating to textiles.

D The **time shifts are very complex** in this poem, and are perhaps **deliberately unclear**. This contributes to the theme of memory, implying a level of **unreliability of memories**.

KEY SETTING: CHURCHYARD (A01)

The poem starts and ends with references to a churchyard and war graves. It opens with a comment about poppies on soldiers' graves, reminding us of the nature of individual suffering, while the final stanza refers to the war memorial, which is more likely to bring to mind ideas of the scale of loss.

KEY THEME: MEMORIES (A02)

Weir presents the speaker's memories as central to the poem using time connectives such as 'before' and 'after'. These connectives join all of her memories together and show how the events are related; in particular how everything is related to Armistice Sunday and to her son's departure.

The use of tense in the poem is another device that supports this theme. Weir employs different past tenses to show different layers of time: the event in line 2 happening longer ago than the one in line 4, for example. This is also part of the texturing she creates in the poem.

KEY TECHNIQUE: SENSE OF TEXTURE

Weir's interest in textiles shines through the poem in her vocabulary choices and imagery, as she introduces physical textures and textiles throughout, from the paper poppy (4–5) to the metaphor of the dove's flight being like a sewing stitch (34) in the final stanza.

The mother's love for the son is also shown through both physical actions and the resisting of them (14), as she is aware of his independence and need for distance. All of this sensory imagery relating to touch helps to root the speaker's highly charged emotional experience in the physical world.

KEY QUOTATION: PHYSICAL MANIFESTATIONS OF CONFLICT

Weir shows the mother's anxiety through the complex textural metaphor of lines 27–8, in which her stomach is represented as cloth being sewn into various complicated folds. As well as fitting within the semantic field of the poem, and contributing to the overall sense of texture, this metaphor conveys a clear sense of the feeling of the stomach twisting and knotting up through uncertainty and concern.

AIMING HIGH: WRITING ABOUT ALTERNATIVE INTERPRETATIONS ⭐

Some readers interpret this poem as suggesting that the son has died, while others see it as simply expressing the mother's feelings about her son's departure for war. Writing about more than one interpretation is a good way to demonstrate flexibility of thinking, but it is crucial to express your ideas tentatively, as possible viewpoints. You should always refer to the poem to provide evidence for any interpretation that you are discussing.

KEY CONTEXT

Poppies have been specifically associated with Armistice Day (11 November, also known as Remembrance Day), the date of the ceasefire that ended the First World War, since the poem 'In Flanders Field' became famous. This moving poem, written in 1915 by John McCrae, refers to poppies and gravesites. Poppies grew across many of the former battlefields in France and Belgium and their red colour is a strong reminder of the blood shed there.

CHECKPOINT 7

What is the effect of the poppy in the first stanza?

Viewpoint: Omniscient third **person** perspective – the narrator knows the photographer's thoughts and feelings.

knowing everything

Theme: The photographer can process his images metaphorically as well as literally when alone.

Structure: Regular rhyming couplets echo the photographer's control when in public.

Key technique: Metaphor of the spools of photographic film conveys emotions locked into the images.

Context: Processing images in a darkroom requires reduced light; only a dim red light does not damage the film.

Theme: Photographer is professional and has a sense of duty.

Theme: Contrast between photographer's experiences at work abroad and at home make the mundane complaints of everyday life seem less severe to him.

Language: Duffy uses the metaphor of the photograph developing in a distorted way to convey the unreality/ haunting nature of the image.

Language: **Juxtaposition** questions the material and emotional cost of the work.

Sound: **Rhyme** trivialises the tears.

Language: **Adverbial** highlights literal suspension in the aeroplane which echoes **metaphorical** suspension between the 'ordinary' world and the conflict.

War Photographer

In his darkroom he is finally alone

with spools of suffering set out in ordered rows.

The only light is red and softly glows,

as though this were a church and he

5 a priest preparing to intone a Mass.

Belfast. Beirut. Phnom Penh. All flesh is grass.

He has a job to do. Solutions slop in trays

beneath his hands, which did not tremble then

though seem to now. Rural England. Home again

10 to ordinary pain which simple weather can dispel,

to fields which don't explode beneath the feet

of running children in a nightmare heat.

Something is happening. A stranger's features

faintly start to twist before his eyes,

15 a half-formed ghost. He remembers the cries

of this man's wife, how he sought approval

without words to do what someone must

and how the blood stained into foreign dust.

A hundred agonies in black-and-white

20 from which his editor will pick out five or six

for Sunday's supplement. The reader's eyeballs prick

with **tears** between the bath and pre-lunch **beers**.

From the aeroplane he stares impassively at where

he earns his living and they do not care.

Colour v1-darkroom

rhyme

onomatopoeia

says with rise/fall words

war torn

rhyme

civilian (human life is brief)

Intro

onomatopoeia

allit

Intro

rhyme

Intro

developing photo

'flickering'

onomatopoeia

dead man

rhyme

blood – dust

(material & emotional)

small emotion

trivialised

showing no emotion

rhyme

desensitised

Suffering

Theme: The photographer keeps his emotions in check when taking pictures, but is unable to suppress his emotion once back home.

Language: **Semantic field** of religion shows photographer's respectful attitude.

Context: Reference to the Bible (Isaiah 40:6) reminds us that human life is brief.

Context: May be a reference to the famous 'Napalm Girl' photograph taken by Nick Ut in Vietnam in 1972.

Theme: Sense of the importance of his work and the respect with which it is carried out.

Form: All stanzas end-stop although there is enjambment within them – part of the poem's control.

Language: **Verb** highlights the small size of the emotional reaction from the reader.

Language: **Irony** shown in final couplet – he has become desensitised through his work and has lost faith in people.

Carol Ann Duffy (b. 1955)

represent or stand for something else
Photographer stands between conflict & reporting experiencing cause & result.

SUMMARY

- A war photographer is developing his pictures in a darkroom under a soft red light.
- The atmosphere is serious and church-like.
- The photographer's hands shake slightly, although they did not when he was in the war zone.
- He remembers the context of each photograph, including a man's wife crying and trying to gain her approval for the picture by meaningful looks.
- He is aware that only a few of his pictures will be published, and that readers will react for just a fleeting moment before continuing with their comfortable lives.

KEY ASPECTS OF THE POEM

A   Duffy uses measured, end-stopped stanzas which **mimic** the photographer's 'ordered' (2) rows.

B   **Contrasts** are established between home and the war zones where he works, and between his understanding and experience and 'the reader' (21) who has become **desensitised**.

KEY SETTING: RURAL ENGLAND   (A02)

Duffy provides little information about the photographer's rural home. The only definite detail that we are told is that it has 'ordinary pain which simple weather can dispel' (10), showing a dismissive attitude through the two **adjectives** 'ordinary' and 'simple'. Duffy makes the photographer view his rural home through the lens of the battlefields he has just left. This is clear through descriptions which focus on what England is not or does not have, rather than on the positive attributes which England may have to offer, such as fields which 'don't explode … in a nightmare heat' (11–12). The effect of this is perhaps to begin to make the English reader ashamed of petty concerns by undercutting them with the more life-threatening events others face.

KEY CONTEXT   (A03)

Carol Ann Duffy (b. 1955) was born in Glasgow and is the first Scottish-born and the first female Poet Laureate. She is a playwright as well as a poet and holds various honours. Her work often focuses on voices that are not usually heard, and she has been criticised for including violence in her poetry, although her work is usually critical of violence.

KEY CONTEXT   (A03)

'All flesh is grass' (5) is a biblical phrase taken from the Old Testament (Isaiah 40:6). It means that human life is brief. Duffy's Catholic upbringing means that biblical and church-related references often occur in her work.

KEY THEME: ATTITUDE TO CONFLICT   (A02)

Duffy contrasts the photographer's haunting memories of war with the reader's sentimental and desensitised reaction to his pictures in the sentence 'The reader's eyeballs prick / with tears between the bath and pre-lunch beers' (21–2). She uses the **verb** 'prick' to show how the tears don't fully emerge and also undermines their seriousness through the **internal rhyme** with 'beers'. A further contrast is offered through the editor, whose job it is to 'pick out five or six' from the 'hundred agonies' (19–20), leaving us to wonder about the cost of such work, where so much suffering is reduced to so few images.

The photographer's attitude, on the other hand, is shown in more complexity. His solemnity is demonstrated through the words 'church', 'priest' and 'Mass' (3–4) and the biblical reference (6), which form a religious *meaningful* ~~semantic~~ field in the first stanza. Duffy also emphasises his sense of duty through repeated references to the idea that he is doing 'what someone must' (17). Although we are not told his specific political views, his attitude that these events must be photographed and made public is made clear.

> **CHECKPOINT 8**   (A03)
>
> What is the significance of 'Belfast. Beirut. Phnom Penh'?

TOP TIP: WRITING ABOUT STRUCTURE   (A02)

Duffy's poem uses a freer metre than many of the older poems in the cluster. Be careful when comparing not to make this sound like a criticism. Several of the more contemporary poems are written to sound more like a natural, conversational voice, but this doesn't mean they 'lack' **rhythm** or are written without **form**. For example, this poem uses regular rhyme but this is not intrusive when read aloud, owing to the **enjambment** and **caesurae**, which create a more conversational rhythm. At the same time, it is worth noting that Duffy has end-stopped each stanza, keeping each contained neatly, like the photographer's 'ordered rows' (2) – this could perhaps be said to show how the photographer is outwardly in control of his emotions, although they do begin to emerge in the privacy of his darkroom.

AIMING HIGH: VOICE AND VIEWPOINT

By using a third person viewpoint, Duffy is able to maintain a certain distance in the poem from both the photographer and the reader. In the final two lines, there is some ambiguity caused by the non-specific references 'where' and 'they', as well as our uncertainty about the adverb 'impassively', which feels uncomfortable when applied to the photographer after being shown that he does care. These ideas are crucial to discuss tentatively as over-assertive claims can be typical of lower level achievement.

more than one meaning – ambiguity

Tissue

Theme: Establishes link between paper and tissue as a key idea.

Key technique: Modal verb of possibility shows potential for change

Voice: Although pronouns are used, overall voice feels impersonal/universal.

Context: Islamic belief part of poet's background.

Theme: Poem reminds us life is short, but records can endure over generations.

Sound: Sibilance evokes gentle, respectful treatment through the soft sound.

Key technique: Conditional clause using subjunctive to show uncertainty; also a structural turning point, from real paper to more abstract/theoretical ideas.

See 'the light' in line 1.

Paper that lets the light

shine through, this

is what could alter things.

Paper thinned by age or touching,

5 the kind you find in well-used books,

the back of the Koran, where a hand

has written in the names and histories,

who was born to whom,

the height and weight, who

10 died where and how, on which sepia date,

pages smoothed and stroked and turned

transparent with attention.

If buildings were paper, I might

feel their drift, see how easily

15 they fall away on a sigh, a shift

in the direction of the wind.

Maps too. The sun shines through

their borderlines, the marks

that rivers make, roads,

20 railtracks, mountainfolds,

Language: Semantic field of light joins several concepts and motifs e.g. fragility, nature, beauty, (im)permanence.

Theme: Paper carries power by storing valuable and precious family records.

Structure: Pace made slow through the repetition of 'and' to convey gentle treatment and respect.

Modal verb – see line 3.

Sound: Irregular rhyme positioning replicates changing wind pattern.

Sound: Alliteration on 'r' and 'm' sounds link these manmade and natural lines as all seeming permanent, while the sun shines on and through them.

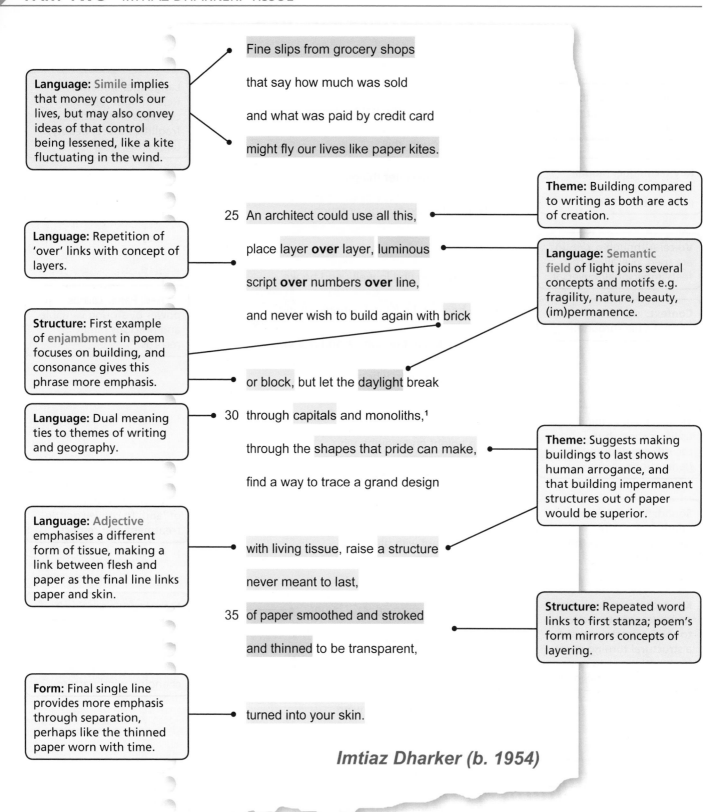

Language: Simile implies that money controls our lives, but may also convey ideas of that control being lessened, like a kite fluctuating in the wind.

Fine slips from grocery shops

that say how much was sold

and what was paid by credit card

might fly our lives like paper kites.

Language: Repetition of 'over' links with concept of layers.

Structure: First example of enjambment in poem focuses on building, and consonance gives this phrase more emphasis.

Language: Dual meaning ties to themes of writing and geography.

Language: Adjective emphasises a different form of tissue, making a link between flesh and paper as the final line links paper and skin.

Form: Final single line provides more emphasis through separation, perhaps like the thinned paper worn with time.

25 An architect could use all this,

place layer **over** layer, luminous

script **over** numbers **over** line,

and never wish to build again with brick

or block, but let the daylight break

30 through capitals and monoliths,[1]

through the shapes that pride can make,

find a way to trace a grand design

with living tissue, raise a structure

never meant to last,

35 of paper smoothed and stroked

and thinned to be transparent,

turned into your skin.

Imtiaz Dharker (b. 1954)

Theme: Building compared to writing as both are acts of creation.

Language: Semantic field of light joins several concepts and motifs e.g. fragility, nature, beauty, (im)permanence.

Theme: Suggests making buildings to last shows human arrogance, and that building impermanent structures out of paper would be superior.

Structure: Repeated word links to first stanza; poem's form mirrors concepts of layering.

Glossary

[1] monolith = a standing stone – also used metaphorically to mean an important structure or institution, particularly one that has been in existence for a long time

SUMMARY

- Paper is presented as having the power to change things, despite its fragility.
- Paper is used in religious texts and to record family history and wears thin over time.
- Other items made of paper record large and small details of life: maps, receipts, plans of buildings.
- The speaker suggests that lives could be constructed or reconstructed out of paper or 'with living tissue' (33), making a connection between paper and human skin.

KEY ASPECTS OF THE POEM

A   Dharker chooses to name the poem 'Tissue', although **paper** is its focus.

B   This poem uses a neutral viewpoint, with a first person perspective.

C   Dharker presents paper, despite being thin and worn, as **possessing power**.

D   The poem is **complex and ambiguous**, its meanings difficult to grasp. Could Dharker be making a point about meaning itself as **fragile and insubstantial**?

KEY THEME: THE POWER OF PAPER   (A01)

Dharker presents paper as powerful in the world because of the ways it can be used, even though the first quality that she emphasises is its thinness and fragility. The thinner the paper is – the more it 'lets the light / shine through' (1–2) – the more powerful it seems to be. Paper is seen as powerful when used for sacred texts such as the Koran, especially when a copy of the text is used to record family history, adding further importance to that book for that family. Dharker also connects cartography (map making), commerce and architecture to paper, referencing key aspects of civilisation.

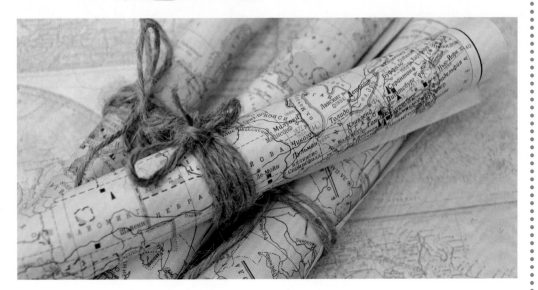

Imtiaz Dharker (b. 1954) was born in Pakistan and moved to Glasgow with her family as a baby. She famously describes herself as a 'Scottish Muslim Calvinist' and her work is often concerned with themes of cultural and geographical movement, freedom and gender. She makes documentary films and is an artist as well as a poet, illustrating her own poetry with line drawings.

Dharker imagines a city 'never meant to last' (34) constructed of layers of paper, made by an architect. This final image running through the last four stanzas shifts between paper and 'living tissue' (33), presenting a shining city that the light can break through and which sems to be embryonic in its development with its thin skin.

AIMING HIGH: DISCUSSING UNCERTAINTY

This poem's complexity offers a good opportunity to demonstrate tentative analysis and handling material with more subtlety. It is useful to be able to show more than one approach to the same text.

One possible interpretation of this poem is that Dharker is commenting on the importance that civilisation places on paper, despite its fragility. Her contrast of paper records and brick buildings may therefore be intended to highlight the vulnerability of written records and perhaps to show that these will not stand the test of time. Alternatively, Dharker can be seen as presenting the power of paper positively, owing to her associations between paper and light. This may also suggest that there would be more light in the world if paper were used for buildings.

KEY TECHNIQUE: UNCERTAIN LANGUAGE

Because this poem has a dream-like quality and explores ideas outside reality, and also because of its theme of how insubstantial things are, Dharker uses language which conveys uncertainty or possibility. There are many **modal verbs** such as 'might' (13) and 'could' (3), and the **conditional** construction 'If buildings were paper' (13) signals that she is writing about things which are imaginary.

REVISION FOCUS: PATTERNS OF LANGUAGE AND IMAGERY

Choose two other poems to compare with 'Tissue' in terms of their use of language or **imagery**. To help you compare them, make a three-line table and write in it: a point explaining the language/imagery you have chosen; a quotation to illustrate your point; some detailed analysis unpicking the effect created. Then add a final sentence or two drawing the poems together.

EXAM FOCUS: WRITING ABOUT POWER

Writing about how a writer uses language to convey the theme of power in a poem is always going to be important. Read this example, which explores Dharker's use of imagery:

Clear focus on writer	Dharker uses the image of 'slips from grocery shops' that 'might fly our lives like paper kites' to perhaps suggest that commerce controls our lives to an unhealthy degree. This image uses two examples of paper to imply that the role of materialism in our lives is ridiculous.	Well-chosen and effectively embedded quotations
Suitably tentative phrasing		Analyses potential meaning
Explains overall impact		

Now you try it:

Write one or two sentences that develop the paragraph further by exploring the image in more depth.

Form: Three equal, end-stopped stanzas, with fairly regular line lengths contribute to a calm, measured tone despite emotive content.

Context: Evokes a woman who has left her country behind.

Viewpoint: First person – direct and personal.

Key technique: Repetition – this is the first mention of a crucial word which concludes each stanza and evokes clarity, brightness and joy.

Theme: Language creates story-like atmosphere, contributing to theme of childhood memories.

Key technique: Metaphor suggests this impression is burnt into the speaker permanently.

Theme: City is associated with light, purity and innocence.

Key technique: Simile of fragility recalls paperweight image in previous stanza, used to suggest her view of her city – it 'cannot break' – whereas the doll is fragile, cannot suppress its feelings.

Key technique: Metaphor shows that her language is a part of her.

Language: Personification of city as placid, wanting speaker to care for it.

Language: Personification changes to a romantic relationship.

Key technique: Ambiguous representation of a city, possibly the one she now lives in, as labyrinthine or divided.

The Emigrée

There once was a country… I left it as a child
but my memory of it is sunlight-clear
for it seems I never saw it in that November
which, I am told, comes to the mildest city.
5 The worst news I receive of it cannot break
my original view, the bright, filled paperweight.
It may be at war, it may be sick with tyrants,
but I am branded by an impression of sunlight.

The white streets of that city, the graceful slopes
10 glow even clearer as time rolls its tanks
and the frontiers rise between us, close like waves.
That child's vocabulary I carried here
like a hollow doll, opens and spills a grammar.
Soon I shall have every coloured molecule of it.
15 It may by now be a lie, banned by the state
but I can't get it off my tongue. It tastes of sunlight.

I have no passport, there's no way back at all
but my city comes to me in its own white plane.
It lies down in front of me, docile as paper;
20 I comb its hair and love its shining eyes.
My city takes me dancing through the city
of walls. They accuse me of absence, they circle me.
They accuse me of being dark in their free city.
My city hides behind me. They mutter death,
25 and my shadow falls as evidence of sunlight.

Carol Rumens (b. 1944)

(handwritten: sight + light; Sounds + language; taste; Insubstantial, Vulnerable to damage; (doll?); touch + movement)

Language: Proper noun 'November' may be a metaphor for the coldness of conflict; by contrast emphasises the exclusively positive nature of speaker's memories.

Key technique: Metaphor of beauty, colour and solidity shows value of memories.

Language: Semantic field with connotations of war over land.

Theme: Hints about what has happened to her culture.

Key technique: Reminiscent of the earlier doll image but here it interacts with the speaker, showing her relationship with her memories/city.

Language: Vague pronoun suggests an unknown or unnamed power, which is threatening.

Language: Metaphor presents the speaker's shadow as proof that there must be light.

Language: Final personification of city as afraid and in need of protection.

CHECKPOINT 9

Why does the emigrée seem to have left her country?

SUMMARY

- The speaker describes having left her country behind when she was a child, but never losing her child-like image of it.
- Whatever bad news she hears of it, she remembers the sunlight and its beauty.
- As an adult, she is becoming aware that this is a false image, but she cannot forget or dismiss this view.
- She cannot return to her city but she is preoccupied by images and fantasies of it.

KEY ASPECTS OF THE POEM

A Rumens uses a range of strong similes and metaphors to present the poem's ideas. These **focus** on the speaker's **memories** of her city, giving the reader a **strong impression** of their clarity and beauty.

B There is a clear first person viewpoint and it is mostly in the present tense.

C The stanzas are all end-stopped and all end with the noun 'sunlight'.

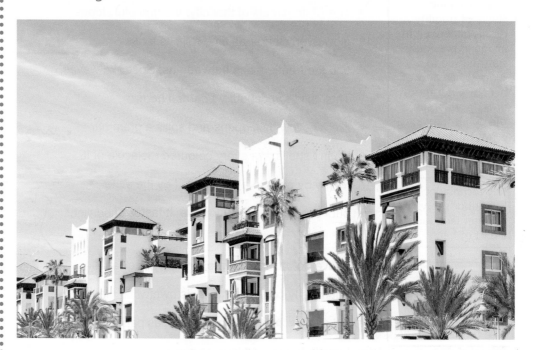

KEY SETTING: THE SPEAKER'S CITY

The speaker's city is presented as full of light, with 'white streets' and 'graceful slopes' (9). Throughout the poem, Rumens focuses on the relationship between the city and the speaker rather than describing it in physical terms. We learn nothing about what the city's buildings are like, for example, nor what landmarks are there, but we do see emotions ascribed to it. Rumens personifies the city as 'docile' (19) at first when it visits the speaker in the final stanza, then more like a lover when it 'takes me dancing' (21) and finally as fearful when it 'hides behind me' (29).

KEY TECHNIQUE: IMAGERY (A02)

This is a poem rich in **imagery**, with strong and complex images to analyse in each stanza. In the first, the deceptively simple metaphor 'my memory of it is sunlight-clear' (2) is worth noting, because it opens a pattern of reference to sunlight which associates the speaker's country with the warmth, cheer and clarity of sunlight, as well as indicating the clarity of the speaker's memories. The more obvious metaphor of 'the bright, filled paperweight' (6) continues this sense of brightness and clarity, as well as adding ideas of value and worth – paperweights are often treasured or valuable objects. It also creates a concept of weight or heaviness through the **adjective** 'filled', which is not strictly necessary and therefore emphasises the idea of the weight of the object, as well as suggesting a paperweight made of glass with bright colours inside. Perhaps the speaker feels weighed down by her memories, but given her insistence on their brightness, this can be only a small part of her experience.

AIMING HIGH: BEING SELECTIVE ⭐

When working with an imagery-rich poem such as this one, do not fall into the trap of trying to analyse everything. It is far better to analyse fully a small selection of images than to try to cover them all and end up making vague or unconnected comments that only scratch the surface. It is sometimes possible to analyse one image in some depth and then mention others as being similar, to demonstrate that you have noticed a pattern of imagery and give an overview. Here, for example, you could discuss 'the bright, filled paperweight' (6) as a metaphor from solidity and also preservation – the objects inside the paperweight preserved in the glass. Its beauty shows the value the speaker attaches to her

memories as well as their vulnerability. This susceptibility to breakage is also present in the 'hollow doll' (13) and 'paper' (19) similes in the second and third stanzas, establishing a clear pattern of the speaker's memories as insubstantial and vulnerable to damage.

KEY QUOTATION: RESISTANCE THROUGH LANGUAGE (A01)

Rumens uses the simile 'That child's vocabulary I carried here / like a hollow doll' (12–13) to show how the speaker's native language was once fragile and not functional but now 'opens and spills a grammar' (13). This indicates how the speaker has embraced this language over time, while the rest of this stanza extends this to show how it is an act of resistance since the language 'may by now be … banned by the state' (15).

KEY CONTEXT (A03)

'Emigrée' is a French noun relating to the English **verb** 'to emigrate'. Compare 'migrate', 'emigrate' and 'immigrate': to migrate is simply to move, with no direction implied, while to emigrate is to leave and to immigrate is to move in. Why do you think Rumens chose the title 'Emigrée' for her poem?

TOP TIP (A02)

This poem is rich in sensory imagery as the speaker imagines and describes a range of interactions between herself and her city. She begins with sight and light, continues with sound and language, then taste, and finally touch and movement, with the city lying down for her to 'comb its hair' (20), dancing with her and hiding behind her. These patterns of imagery are part of how Rumens constructs a sense of the speaker's memories and her relationship with those memories.

Key technique: Phonetic spelling showing Caribbean dialect to create a clear identity.

Key technique: Juxtaposition of pronouns to show how the speaker is taking back power from 'dem'.

Language: Metaphors of imposed visual impairment demonstrate that being kept ignorant of history is disabling.

Key technique: Repetition to show dullness of history that was taught in the UK, ignoring Black history.

Theme: Power is maintained by telling certain stories and keeping people ignorant of some versions or aspects of history.

Context: French emperor and military leader. Led the armies who fought Nelson at the Battle of Trafalgar and Wellington at the Battle of Waterloo, famous moments in British history (see line 32).

Language: Plain, factual style for the British history contrasts with the more imagery-rich Caribbean material.

Language: The phrase 'see-far' suggests she was a truth-teller/ahead of her time.

Checking Out Me History

Dem tell me

Dem tell me

Wha dem want to tell me

Bandage up me eye with me own history

5   Blind me to me own identity

Dem tell me bout 1066 and all dat

dem tell me bout Dick Whittington and he cat

But Toussaint L'Ouverture[1]

no dem never tell me bout dat

10   *Toussaint*

         a slave

         with vision

         lick back

         Napoleon

15   *battalion*

         and first Black

         Republic born

         Toussaint de thorn

         to de French

20   *Toussaint de beacon*

         of de Haitian Revolution

Dem tell me bout de man who discover de balloon

and de cow who jump over de moon

Dem tell me bout de dish ran away with de spoon

25 but dem never tell me bout Nanny de Maroon[2]

         Nanny

         see-far woman

Voice: First person speaker with a strong Caribbean-British identity.

Theme: History is a construction put together by those in power.

Language: Possessives show sense of taking back what already belongs to the speaker.

Theme: Sense of British history as set of dates that everyone is supposed to know.

Theme: Examples of British history include folk tales, i.e. unreal 'events', showing uselessness of what was taught.

Form: Italics and indents used to highlight Caribbean history, written in more lyrical style.

Language: Metaphor linked to nature shows how Toussaint was a problem to the French in freeing Haiti.

Language: Imagery of light used throughout Caribbean sections perhaps symbolising hope and truth.

Form: Rhyme used frequently but not a strict scheme as poem is free verse; here rhyme creates mocking effect with childish vowel sound on every line.

Structure: Layout and style clearly present Caribbean and British history as distinct.

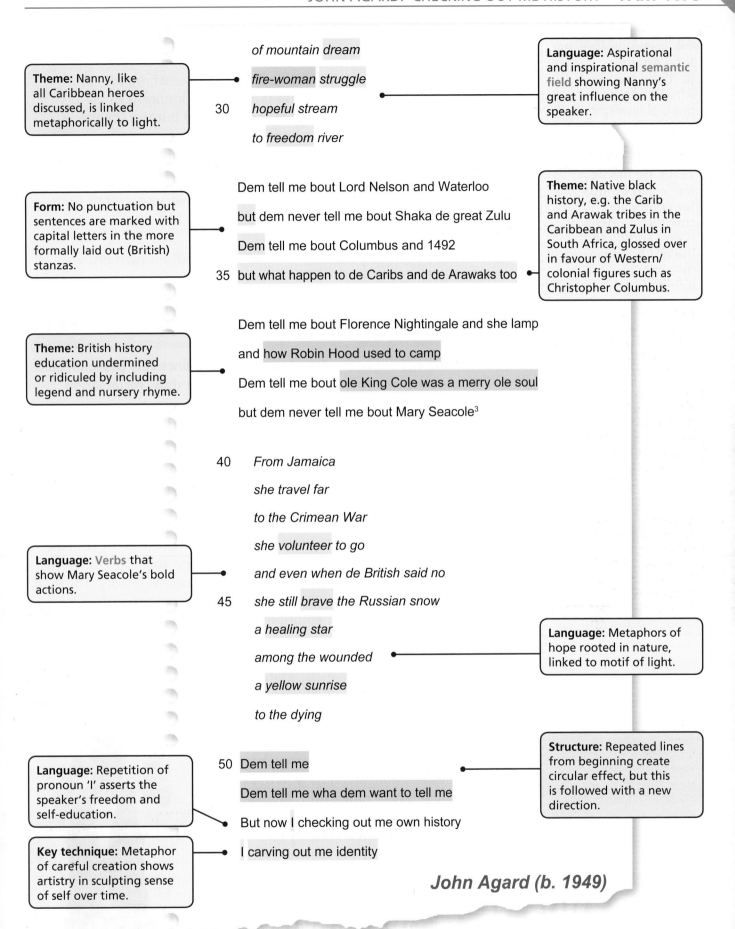

Theme: Nanny, like all Caribbean heroes discussed, is linked metaphorically to light.

of mountain dream

fire-woman struggle

30   hopeful stream

to freedom river

Language: Aspirational and inspirational semantic field showing Nanny's great influence on the speaker.

Form: No punctuation but sentences are marked with capital letters in the more formally laid out (British) stanzas.

Dem tell me bout Lord Nelson and Waterloo

but dem never tell me bout Shaka de great Zulu

Dem tell me bout Columbus and 1492

35   but what happen to de Caribs and de Arawaks too

Theme: Native black history, e.g. the Carib and Arawak tribes in the Caribbean and Zulus in South Africa, glossed over in favour of Western/colonial figures such as Christopher Columbus.

Theme: British history education undermined or ridiculed by including legend and nursery rhyme.

Dem tell me bout Florence Nightingale and she lamp

and how Robin Hood used to camp

Dem tell me bout ole King Cole was a merry ole soul

but dem never tell me bout Mary Seacole[3]

40   From Jamaica

she travel far

to the Crimean War

she volunteer to go

and even when de British said no

Language: Verbs that show Mary Seacole's bold actions.

45   she still brave the Russian snow

a healing star

among the wounded

a yellow sunrise

to the dying

Language: Metaphors of hope rooted in nature, linked to motif of light.

Language: Repetition of pronoun 'I' asserts the speaker's freedom and self-education.

50   Dem tell me

Dem tell me wha dem want to tell me

But now I checking out me own history

Key technique: Metaphor of careful creation shows artistry in sculpting sense of self over time.

I carving out me identity

Structure: Repeated lines from beginning create circular effect, but this is followed with a new direction.

John Agard (b. 1949)

Glossary

1   Toussaint L'Ouverture = Haitian revolutionary who worked to abolish slavery, and then in Haiti to free it from French rule
2   Nanny de (the) Maroon = a Jamaican national heroine who fought against slavery
3   Mary Seacole = a Jamaican nurse in the Crimean War

KEY CONTEXT   **A03**

John Agard (b. 1949) is an Afro-Guyanese poet, playwright and children's writer who has lived in Britain since the 1970s. He has won numerous awards for poetry and children's books and is well known for his use of Caribbean dialect in his writing.

SUMMARY

- The speaker explains what teachers have been teaching him as 'history' (4) and expresses a sense that he feels ignorant of his 'own identity' (5). This identity is not explicitly stated but the speaker is implicitly presented as a Caribbean British man.
- He lists key – but distant – dates in British history, nursery rhymes and folk tales as things that he has been taught.
- He also gives information about Toussaint L'Ouverture, Nanny the Maroon and Mary Seacole, all iconic Caribbean historical figures about whom he was never taught.
- He ends by declaring that he is finding out about his own history for himself.

KEY ASPECTS OF THE POEM

A   Agard uses Caribbean **dialect** to create a **distinctively personal** voice.

B   He contrasts the **pronouns** 'dem' and 'me' to show **reclamation of power**.

C   The poem's **structure** shows Caribbean history as **separate** from European.

KEY SETTING: ENGLAND   **A01**

England is implicitly presented as a colonial power, imposing its history on the speaker, regardless of his Caribbean heritage. The culture of England is summarised through a mixture of nursery rhymes and folk tales as well as more traditional history, none of which represents recent history. The idea that this history is put together through choice and could therefore have been constructed differently is emphasised through Agard's insistence that 'Dem tell me wha dem want to tell me' (51).

KEY THEME: IDENTITY   **A02**

Agard presents history as key to understanding identity. He uses Caribbean dialect, such as 'dem' in place of 'they', as one way of presenting an authentic British-Caribbean identity in this poem. The poem explains how only British history and culture has been taught, so the speaker is 'checking out' (52) Caribbean history for himself. There is a clear sense that the speaker's history and identity have been deliberately withheld from him, presented through the **metaphors** in the second stanza. Agard describes the speaker as 'bandage[d]' (4) and 'blind[ed]' (5), showing that he experiences this lack of knowledge of his own history as a kind of disability.

The way that the new-found pieces of history are presented shows how they are valued by the speaker. They are set apart from the rest of the poem by being in italics and indented, but the **tone** in which they are told is also different. The English history and culture is all presented in a very bland, factual way, but the Caribbean material is much more lyrical, using metaphors such as 'Toussaint de thorn / to de French' (18–19), implying how Toussaint was an irritation to the French armies. Similarly, Mary Seacole is described as 'a healing star / among the wounded / a yellow sunrise / to the dying' (46–9), as opposed to the other famous Crimean War nurse 'Florence Nightingale and she lamp' (36). The metaphors describing Mary Seacole help to show how the speaker values his Caribbean identity, as they create a sense of her value by associating her with the stars and the sun.

CHECKPOINT 10 (A01)

Why does Agard give us information about Toussaint l'Ouverture, Nanny the Maroon and Mary Seacole, but only mentions in passing all the figures from British history and culture?

KEY QUOTATION: CREATING AN IDENTITY (A02)

In the final stanza, Agard shows the speaker's determination through the metaphor 'I carving out me identity' (50), telling us that this new identity will be crafted, sculpted from hard materials and built to last. The metaphor also suggests that this identity is something that he is taking time to make, digging it out layer by layer. It implies that each new piece of history that he discovers adds something to his identity, building it gradually. Agard suggests that identity is not something that can be constructed in an instant or imposed from the outside.

REVISION FOCUS: IDENTITY

Which other poems do you think concern the theme of identity? Make a list of the ways in which identity is explored throughout the cluster, noting all the poems that you think are relevant, in addition to 'Checking Out Me History'. Then choose two other poems that you feel are most relevant to the theme of identity. Write a paragraph for each of these three poems in which you select and explain one quotation which relates to this theme.

Context: 'Kamikaze' refers to a Japanese practice in the Second World War where an aeroplane was loaded with explosives and flown into a target, killing the pilot as well as destroying the target.

Kamikaze

Viewpoint: The poem's initial narrator is third **person** and is unconnected to events.

Her father embarked at sunrise

with a flask of water, a samurai sword

in the cockpit, a shaven head

magic spell/chant

full of powerful incantations

Key technique: Storyteller-like **tone** has a distancing effect.

Key technique: Ambiguity may refer to propaganda, prayers or his own thoughts.

Context: Being selected to be a kamikaze pilot was a great honour and the men's families were respected afterwards.

5   and enough fuel for a one-way

journey into history

Viewpoint: Speaker reveals daughter's thoughts here – a switch from the first stanza.

Key technique: Distance created by using different **voices**, since the pilot cannot tell anyone his thoughts.

but half way there, she thought,

recounting it later to her children,

Language: Verbs show she is imagining and interpreting his reasons, which also creates distance from the reader.

he must have looked far down

10   at the little fishing boats

strung out like bunting

semi transparent

on a green-blue translucent sea

Theme: Single event has a long-term effect, interesting and affecting future generations.

Language: Simile evokes celebration and joy.

Language: Sea described with beauty, emphasising colour and light.

Waves rows?

Language: Simile suggests patriotism, pride or celebration.

and beneath them, arcing in swathes

like a huge flag waved first one way

15   then the other in a figure of eight,

Language: Fish can be seen as metaphors for the planes, responding to Japan's (the sun's) orders – in this context, 'dark' becomes more sinister.

the dark shoals of fishes

flashing silver as their bellies

swivelled towards the sun

Sound: Harmonious consonance evokes pleasing, rapid movement.

Context: Echoes the Japanese flag, which depicts a red circle on a white background. Japan was known as the 'land of the rising sun' because of its easterly position.

Theme: Power of memory; there is a change of ideas with each new stanza, emphasised by the **enjambment**.

and remembered how he and

20   his brothers waiting on the shore

built cairns[1] of pearl-grey pebbles

to see whose withstood longest

churned up

Language: Ambiguity – implication that the idea of waiting for his father may be what prompts him to return to his family.

the turbulent inrush of breakers

bringing their father's boat safe

Language: Waves can be seen as a metaphor for the war and perhaps the pilot's decision.

✳

Speaking to her children

Form: Italics mark shift to the daughter's voice speaking directly to her children.

Language: Sensory description conveys specific and physical details of fish caught to emphasise richness of sea-life.

Structure: Key turning point marked by first full stop preceding this, and main shift in voice to the first person.

Voice: Daughter speaking directly here about her family's behaviour.

Theme: Conforming with society, perhaps despite her inclinations.

Language: Use of conditional showing they knew he did return, but had to pretend that he did not.

Key technique: Reported speech adds another clear layer of distance to this complex last thought, zooming out again at the end of the poem.

25 *– yes, grandfather's boat – safe*

to the shore, salt-sodden, awash

with cloud-marked mackerel,

black crabs, feathery prawns,

the loose silver of whitebait and once

30 *a tuna, the dark prince, muscular, dangerous.*

And though he came back

my mother never spoke again

in his presence, nor did she meet his eyes

and the neighbours too, they treated him

35 *as though he no longer existed,*

only we children still chattered and laughed

till gradually we too learned

to be silent, to live as though

he had never returned, that this

40 *was no longer the father we loved.*

And sometimes, she said, he must have wondered

which had been the better way to die. *alienated.*

by community — a death

Language: Grandiose and metaphorical description of the tuna seems foreboding.

first full stop

Theme: Shame culture and its use of punishment through the entire community.

Language: The daughter shows empathy for her father and expresses past feelings but her emotions seem complex.

Language: Verbs show the pilot's daughter is imagining what he thought but the past tense shows she cannot ask.

Language: Metaphorical (social) as well as literal death: the father reflected on whether it would have been better to die in his plane, rather than this slow death of being alienated by his community.

Beatrice Garland (b. 1938)

p 68

Glossary

¹ Cairns = burial or memorial place markers constructed out of stones, often circular

Beatrice Garland (b. 1938) is an Oxford-born poet, NHS clinician and teacher who won the National Poetry Prize in 2001. She has written poetry on a wide range of subjects, but people's attitudes to and treatment of one another is a common theme.

SUMMARY

- An unnamed woman's father left on a kamikaze mission when she was a girl but did not complete it.
- The woman explains to her children why he returned, guessing what he may have thought.
- She imagines that he saw fishing boats, thought of his own family's boats and remembered his childhood.
- His wife did not speak to him on his return, nor did his neighbours, and the children learned to ignore him as well, so his daughter does not really know what he may have been thinking.
- However, the poem ends with her surmising that he may have regretted his decision after the community isolated him.

KEY ASPECTS OF THE POEM

A The description and imagery relating to fishing and the sea **evoke a strong sense of place and family**.

B Two distinct voices are created: the speaker's and that of the daughter herself. The father's **lack of voice** is also important.

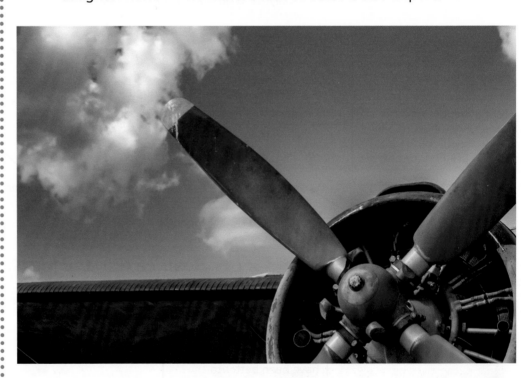

KEY SETTING: THE SEA   **A01**

Garland presents the sea as beautiful in its own right. She emphasises both colour and light in creating the setting, making it clear how such an image might well have persuaded the pilot to abandon his mission and live. The picture built up of the sea teeming with all its life (16–18) is one of hope, and as readers we can understand how the pilot could have been reminded of a childhood on the shore building piles of stones (21). It is also significant that Garland chooses a noun signifying a burial mound or place of ceremonial value that the pilot remembers building, rather than simply a heap of stones. This may contrast with the life-affirming imagery of the fish in the waters, or it may imply ritualistic games of waiting for their father to return from the sea.

KEY CONTEXT A03

Post-war Japanese society was very rigid socially, with extremely strict and complex rules governing many social exchanges. The concept of honour – and its opposite, shame – was crucial as a motivating factor in decisions, including social interactions.

KEY TECHNIQUE: CREATING DISTANCE

The speaker's and daughter's voices are both used to create distance, which supports the poem's theme and main concept of a shunned returned kamikaze pilot. The speaker's voice creates a fairytale-like effect at the start by using the third **person** past **tense**, which has a neutral, distant tone. This distance is further increased when the speaker is reporting indirectly what the daughter recounted to her children (8). Another effect of this is to prepare us for the fact that we are reading suppositions, as we cannot know what the father was thinking since nobody spoke to him after his return.

The daughter's voice is presented directly by using italics, but again distance is created since she speaks about what her mother and the neighbours did, rather than sharing her own thoughts and feelings directly. This distance also helps to present the conflict in an indirect way, which is appropriate in this context.

AIMING HIGH: HOW IS THE FATHER PRESENTED?

This is a complex poem that presents a complex set of attitudes. You therefore have the opportunity to demonstrate your skill in making tentative suggestions of possible interpretations, and supporting them clearly with evidence from the poem. It is clear by the end that the daughter's prevailing emotion is sympathy for her father, and perhaps guilt for how he has been treated. We can see this in the final two lines, where complex **verbs** create a huge distance between her and the realisation of what his life was like, being so isolated from his family – she wonders if her father thought dying as a pilot might have been better than dying alone. The mass of verbs in lines 41–2 also shows us that it is too late – whichever would have been better, the last line is so definitely past tense that there is no chance of recovery.

PROGRESS AND REVISION CHECK

SECTION ONE: CHECK YOUR KNOWLEDGE

Answer these quick questions to test your basic knowledge of the poems.

1. Which poet uses a semantic field related to textiles?

2. Which poem features Mary Seacole?

3. Which poem refers to the 'cold clockwork of the stars'?

4. What is the difference between an emigrée and an immigrant?

5. Who is described as 'king of kings'?

6. Name the two types of enemy in 'The Charge of the Light Brigade'.

7. In 'Tissue', what is written in the back of the Koran?

8. Which poem is all about a painting?

9. Which poem begins 'We are prepared'?

10. In which poem do people move 'half a league'?

11. Who organises 'spools of suffering' into 'ordered rows'?

12. Name two buildings that are mentioned in 'London'.

13. Name two gifts that the Duchess liked 'too easily'.

14. Which poem shows sympathy for the French Revolution?

15. Name three body parts which are described in 'Ozymandias'.

16. Which poem features a hare?

17. What famously happens in 'Exposure'?

18. What frightens the boy in the extract from, 'The Prelude'?

19. Name two types of fish in 'Kamikaze'.

20. Which poem ends 'his bloody life in my bloody hands'?

SECTION TWO: CHECK YOUR UNDERSTANDING

Here are two tasks about the significance of certain moments in two poems. These require more thought and longer responses. In each case try to write at least three to four paragraphs.

Task 1: How does Jane Weir use texture in 'Poppies', and how do the images she chooses relate to the speaker's feelings? Think about:

- The techniques the poet uses
- How these techniques create effects

Task 2: How does Alfred Lord Tennyson convey the action of the battlefield in 'The Charge of the Light Brigade'? Think about:

- The structure, rhythm and rhyme of the poem
- How these create effects

PROGRESS CHECK

GOOD PROGRESS

I can:

- Understand how each poem has a different voice or viewpoint and ideas to express. ☐
- Select well-chosen evidence, including key quotations, to support my ideas. ☐

EXCELLENT PROGRESS

I can:

- Analyse how the poets have used a range of techniques to create voices and convey ideas. ☐
- Draw on a range of carefully selected key evidence, including quotations, to support my ideas. ☐

THEMES

SOCIAL STRUCTURES AND POWER

Social structure and organisation is a traditional literary concern, and many authors have written about how power is managed within society, whether by individual leaders or through systems of social rule such as a democracy, dictatorship or socialism. Power structures can be presented within a country or reflected within a single household.

Several poems in the cluster offer ideas about power in social organisation:

- In **'Ozymandias'**, Shelley presents the arrogance of rulership through the statue's features such as its 'sneer of cold command' (5). He also undermines this power by showing its transitory nature, since the civilisation that the statue celebrates no longer exists, making the bold claims on its plaque both **ironic** and pitiful.

- In **'London'**, Blake's presentation of social structure is perhaps less explicit, but he singles out the lower classes for sympathy, and contrasts these with the more powerful. Blake also implies that the higher classes are corrupt and use their power to oppress people like 'the chimney-sweeper' (9) and 'the hapless soldier' (11).

- Browning is the only poet in the cluster to take on the **voice** of an upper-class character, through a **dramatic monologue**, although **'My Last Duchess'** is plainly critical of the Duke's rigid perspective on class.

- In **'My Last Duchess'**, Browning guides the reader to perceive that the Duke's interpretation of the Duchess's behaviour is unreasonable and his statement 'I choose / Never to stoop' (41–2) casts him in a negative light as excessively focused on the power he holds in society above all else.

- **'Checking Out Me History'** also has this theme at its root, as the British Empire is effectively a specific kind of power structure. Without it, the choices about the speaker's education would not have been made for him.

- **'The Emigrée'** touches on this theme through the mentions of the changes made in the speaker's country, such as her language being 'banned by the state' (15), although these are presented as possibilities rather than absolute certainties, perhaps reflecting the difficulties of receiving reliable news from countries in crisis.

KEY QUOTATION: TREATING EACH ACCORDING TO THEIR RANK (A01)

Browning indicates the Duke's belief that the Duchess should have treated people differently, according to their social status, when he remarks 'but who passed without / Much the same smile?' (44–5) This rhetorical question shows his incredulity that she could treat others of a lower status in the same way as him.

RESISTING OPPRESSION

One of literature's traditional purposes is 'speaking back' against oppression, whether to draw attention to it, to express anger about it or to encourage rebellion. A few poems in this cluster express resistance against unfair use of power:

- **'Checking Out Me History'** does so most clearly and is itself an act of resistance, with the speaker trying to put right the imbalance in his education. Agard reclaims power from 'dem' – white educators and society – by giving prominence to Caribbean historical figures.

- In **'London'**, Blake's references to black and red link to the French Revolution, reminding contemporary readers of the possibility of violent resistance.

- In **'The Emigrée'**, Rumens shows a kind of passive resistance, since her memories of her homeland cannot be taken from her, no matter how power is abused in her country.

- **'The Charge of the Light Brigade'** offers a counterpoint, since it emphasises the soldiers' lack of resistance and their loyalty in simply following orders: 'Theirs not to reason why, / Theirs but to do and die' (14–15).

THEME TRACKER (A01)

Resisting oppression

- 'Checking Out Me History': Finding out about Caribbean history is an act of rebellion to redress the imbalance in the history taught to the speaker.

- 'London': The speaker hints at a possible revolution to come.

- 'The Emigrée': The emigrée's memories cannot be taken from her.

EXAM FOCUS: WRITING ABOUT POWER (A02)

You may be asked to compare how poets present power in 'Checking Out Me History' and another poem. Read this example, which chooses 'The Emigrée' and focuses on the theme of resistance:

Embedded quotations	Agard firmly contrasts 'wha dem' taught with 'me own history', using Caribbean dialect and the possessive 'own' to put 'dem' firmly in their place as an act of resistance. He could go into detail about 'dem', expressing hatred or anger, but the dismissive pronoun is enough to show that the speaker is not allowing them any power in this poem. Rumens also uses a contrast in her poem, using certainty and uncertainty to show how she cannot be separated from her memories, no matter what. When she writes about what has happened to her city since she left, she uses modal verbs such as 'may', showing that she is uncertain about what has happened. Her statements about her memories, however, are all much more definite: 'I am branded by an impression of sunlight.'

Correct terminology

Explains effect of language choices

Compares language technique

Explains meaning but could link to theme here

Good use of terminology

Now you try it:

Improve this paragraph by adding a concluding sentence or two to bring it back to the topic of resistance.

THEME TRACKER **A01**

Social control

- 'My Last Duchess': the Duke has the Duchess killed when she fails to follow his unspoken rules.

- 'Kamikaze': the pilot is shunned by his community when he fails to complete his mission.

- 'Checking Out Me History': the version of history taught to the speaker is a form of social control that puts White British culture in power.

SOCIAL CONTROL

Several poems in the cluster present ways in which social control is managed:

- In **'My Last Duchess'**, the Duke believes that the Duchess should know how she is supposed to behave without him having to 'stoop' (34) to tell her. When that fails, the Duke uses his power to get rid of her: 'I gave commands. / Then all smiles stopped together' (45–6).

- In **'Kamikaze'**, we see how when a society shuns an individual the effects are profound: here, a pilot is ostracised for failing to complete a suicide mission.

- The social control shown in **'Checking Out Me History'** concerns the educational choices made by the former British Empire. Agard suggests that a traditional curriculum, as shown in the poem, helps to maintain the concept of White Britain as all-powerful.

RESPONSIBILITY

The concept of responsibility is a key literary theme associated with power and conflict, and various poems in the cluster reference it in different ways:

- In **'London'**, Blake implies that the 'church' (10) and the 'palace' (12) should bear responsibility for the chimney-sweeper's and soldier's miserable and dangerous situations.

- In **'Remains'**, Armitage uses repetitive phrasing and ideas to show how the soldier is haunted by his own sense of responsibility for the life he contributed to taking.

- In Duffy's **'War Photographer'**, the photographer is full of a sense of duty: he does 'what someone must' (17). Responsibility is what keeps him doing his job despite its obvious difficulties.

- In **'The Charge of the Light Brigade'**, Tennyson mentions that 'Some one had blunder'd' (12) but focuses more upon the soldiers' sense of duty and responsibility – they do what is asked of them.

THEME TRACKER **A01**

Responsibility

- 'London': Blake suggests institutions representing the higher classes should take responsibility for looking after the lower classes.

- 'Remains': the responsibility for taking a life is shown to be too much.

- 'War Photographer': the speaker suggests that showing the world what is happening in war zones is a duty.

KEY QUOTATION: PLACING THE BLAME **A01**

Blake presents the chimney-sweep's plight as a direct accusation of the Church in the lines telling us that the speaker hears 'How the chimney-sweeper's cry / Every black'ning church appalls' (9–10). This shows that the Church is responsible for not alleviating the chimney-sweeper's situation, with the 'black'ning' becoming a metaphorical stain of shame for this.

WAR – PARTICIPATION

Several of the poems in the cluster describe direct experience of war:

- In **'Exposure'**, soldiers in the First World War wait while 'nothing happens' (6). Owen makes it clear that inaction was frequent and his vivid description of the weather and conditions shows how the soldiers were at risk not just from bullets, gas and shells.

- In **'Bayonet Charge'**, a soldier rises to charge, but is struck with indecision, before plunging ahead once more. Hughes shows that following orders, while dangerous, is probably safer and feels more comfortable than thinking for oneself on the battlefield.

- In **'Remains'**, Armitage offers a haunting vision of the reality of having to kill someone. Despite three soldiers being involved, the speaker is left with the recurring image of 'his bloody life in my bloody hands' (30).

- In **'The Charge of the Light Brigade'**, Tennyson evokes the atmosphere of the battlefield and emphasises the risks taken by soldiers.

WAR – BEING LEFT BEHIND

Other poems in this cluster address aspects of war experienced by those not actually fighting:

- In **'Poppies'**, Weir compares a mother's memories of the day her son leaves for war with her earlier memories of his childhood.

- **'The Charge of the Light Brigade'** has a more official **tone** to it, seeming to command its audience how to respond: 'Honour the Light Brigade' (54).

- **'War Photographer'** discusses the desensitisation of the masses to images of war in the media. Duffy presents the public as an unmoved audience who 'do not care' (24) for more than a brief moment about the horrors shown in the 'spools of suffering' (2).

- In **'Kamikaze'**, it is those left behind who judge and punish the pilot when he does not carry out his mission. His daughter's uncertainty about his motivation leads the reader also to wonder exactly what his experience was.

AIMING HIGH: WRITING ABOUT WAR ⭐

There are many different possible angles in writing about war and conflict. Addressing more than one angle can be a good way to show all-round knowledge of the poems and cover a wider range of poetic techniques. For example, if writing about 'experiences of conflict', you could contrast a poem about battle experience with one about being left behind. This approach can give you a wider choice of poems for comparison and introduce broader contrasts in language techniques if, for example, you compare older and newer poems.

THEME TRACKER (A01)

War – participation

- 'Exposure': waiting around in poor conditions is another danger for the soldiers.

- 'Bayonet Charge': a soldier hesitates on the battlefield, but quickly resumes following orders.

- 'Remains': despite training, and the security of others taking the same action, killing another person has a profound effect on the speaker.

THEME TRACKER (A01)

War – being left behind

- 'Poppies': a mother remembers seeing her son off to war.

- 'The Charge of the Light Brigade': the audience is told how to respond to the soldiers.

- 'War Photographer': the public's desensitisation to war images is lamented.

THEME TRACKER (A01)

Attitudes to war

● 'Exposure': the soldiers have had enough and are waiting for it to be over.

● 'The Charge of the Light Brigade': the speaker urges the audience to 'honour' the Light Brigade.

● 'War Photographer': the public has become uncaring about images of war.

ATTITUDES TO WAR

Various poems in the cluster display different attitudes to war:

● '**Exposure**' offers us the weary attitude of soldiers in the trenches in the second half of the First World War, when everything seemed hopeless and they felt as much at risk from the elements as from the enemy.

● '**The Charge of the Light Brigade**' displays a strongly positive attitude towards the soldiers themselves, as Tennyson exhorts us to 'honour' (53) them. We also see the Light Brigade willingly enter 'the valley of Death' (3), a phrase chosen to evoke loyalty and faith as well as the certainty of death.

● In Duffy's '**War Photographer**', the photographer has a professional attitude to working in a war zone, controlling his feelings in order to 'do what someone must' (17), but his real emotions escape when he develops his photographs back home. In contrast, the people looking at the photographs are somewhat unfeeling, responding emotionally only very briefly, thus presenting the idea that the public have become desensitised to war.

● '**Bayonet Charge**' shows relatively complex attitudes to war through the soldier's indecision. Ultimately, it's easier – and safer – for him to resume following orders and relinquish control to his commanders. We can see that the soldier's own feelings about what he should or should not be doing become unimportant and almost dangerous.

● '**Kamikaze**' reveals attitudes within a specific community with its own notions of convention and honour about how war should be fought, since nobody will acknowledge the presence of the returned kamikaze pilot.

THEME TRACKER (A01)

The effects of war

● 'Remains': psychological effects on an individual of having to kill.

● 'Kamikaze': social effects on an individual who failed to follow orders.

● 'The Emigrée': after-effects of fleeing a land in conflict.

THE EFFECTS OF WAR

The after-effects of war are explored in several poems in the cluster:

● In '**Remains**', Armitage demonstrates the psychological damage endured by an individual.

● Garland's '**Kamikaze**' also considers the effects on an individual, but this time the social effects of his decision are the focus.

● In '**The Emigrée**', the effects shown all take place after a family has fled a country in conflict.

● In '**Poppies**', Weir shows us the effects in a more subtle way by focusing on the family, specifically the mother, of a soldier going off to war.

REVISION FOCUS: COMPARING WAR POEMS

Make a paper list of all the poems in the cluster that relate to war. Cut it up, shuffle the titles and draw out two at random. Challenge yourself to make at least **five comparisons** between these poems. Some of your points should focus on what the poems say about war (their theme or content) and some on how they say it (use of language, form and structure). Remember that comparisons can show differences as well as similarities.

NATURE

Nature is an important theme in poetry as a whole, and many poems address the concepts of the power of nature or the conflict between man and nature. These ideas are both explored by poems in this cluster:

- In the extract from, '**The Prelude**', Wordsworth shows the beauty and grandeur of nature when the boy is first rowing out and notices details like the 'small circles glittering idly' (9). Although the boy is pleased with his own strength in rowing, nature has the power to seize his attention. Wordsworth displays the truly awesome power of nature in the 'huge' (22) and terrifying peak which frightens the boy so much that it spoils his memory of the adventure.

- Conflict between man and nature is also evident in '**The Prelude**', as Wordsworth presents the peak as chasing the boy.

- Heaney's '**Storm on the Island**' shows the power of nature to destroy. He presents the storm as attacking the houses, going from 'pummel[ing]' (10) to 'bombard[ing]' (19).

- The idea of conflict with nature is clear in Heaney's description of preparing for the storm. The speaker in his poem knows the storm will attack, and while the people do all they can in terms of building a certain way and waiting, they cannot prevent or fight back against it.

- Owen shows in '**Exposure**' how dangerous nature can be, since here it is the weather conditions that are killing off the soldiers, not the battle. They see the air as 'deadly' (18), with the chill it brings, rather than the bullets.

- In '**Ozymandias**', nature has wiped away a ruler's empire. There are no remnants of Ozymandias's great nation, only the 'lone and level sands' (14), showing that however great humans' power, nature is greater in the end.

TOP TIP: WRITING ABOUT SECONDARY THEMES (A01)

Always remember to keep the focus of your question in mind in your answer. Secondary themes such as nature may be relevant, depending on which poems you are analysing, but they should not form the primary focus of your answer unless your question is about them. You have limited time in the exam and no examiner expects you to cover everything that it is possible to say about the poems in that time: you must prioritise in order to answer your question effectively.

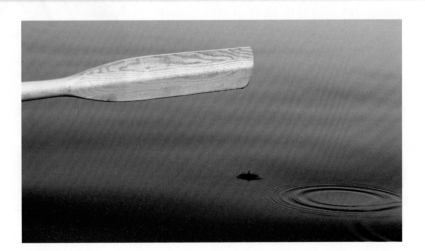

THEME TRACKER (A01)

Nature

- Extract from, 'The Prelude': nature can be both beautiful and terrifyingly powerful.

- 'Storm on the Island': nature, in the form of storms, is unstoppable and vicious.

- 'Exposure': nature, in the form of wintry conditions, is just as deadly than gunfire.

CHECKPOINT 12 (A01)

Which poem uses a **simile** comparing the sea to a 'tame cat turned savage'?

Memory

- 'Remains': the soldier's experience is constantly relived as an unwanted memory.

- Extract from 'The Prelude': the boy's memory of his adventure is spoilt by the 'huge peak' (22).

- 'The Emigrée': the speaker's memories of her country are a treasured possession.

MEMORY

The idea of memories and how people are affected by them is a well-established literary theme, for novels and plays as well as poetry. Several of the poems in this cluster concern themselves with this idea:

- In '**Remains**', the effect on the speaker's mental health of the memory recalled is the central theme. He is unable to erase the incident from his mind and is constantly haunted by images and thoughts relating to it. Armitage presents the dead man as physically present with the soldier – 'he's here' (25) – and lists the various ways in which he haunts him, emphasising the speaker's inability to stop the memory replaying.

- Similarly, the extract from, '**The Prelude**' concludes with the idea that the boy's next few days and nights after the episode are haunted by the incident and he is unable to take any pleasure from it.

- On the other hand, a positive presentation of memory is offered in '**The Emigrée**', where the speaker's memories are seen as a treasured possession which cannot be taken from her.

- In '**Poppies**', Weir uses the speaker's earlier memories as a structural device. They are interwoven with memories of the son's departure for war as a means of presenting the relationship between mother and son and to show her thoughts and feelings.

KEY QUOTATION: ATTITUDE TO MEMORIES (A01)

In 'The Emigrée', Rumens presents the speaker's memories of her home city as a 'bright, filled paperweight' (6) and tells us that 'The worst news I receive of it cannot break / my original view' (5–6). This indicates the great value that the speaker places on her memories and also shows how invested in them she is. She is unable to change her idea of the place, no matter what she hears about it, even though the metaphor she has chosen is a breakable object – a 'filled paperweight' implies a glass outer. This shows a strongly protective attitude towards the memories of her home.

ART

Art and poetry are linked concepts, so it is not unusual to find poets writing about the nature of art. A few of the poems in this cluster touch on ideas relating to art and visual images:

- **'My Last Duchess'** is about a painting that shows an image of the Duchess that the Duke can be happy with, since he became disappointed with the live woman, when he found he had less power over her than he would have liked. The reference to 'Neptune … cast in bronze' (54–6) shows the Duke's taste for art that demonstrates masculine power, as Neptune is depicted 'taming a sea-horse' (55).

- In **'War Photographer'**, Duffy shows a professional developing images of war to show to the public. The poem explores the role of art – in this case photography – as a means of representing life, and an audience's response to it. Photography here has become art, which has become a commodity. The photographer, although he provides the images for this process, does not have this as his intention – he wants people to understand. His editor, however, is less concerned about understanding the context of conflict than about provoking a reaction from the audience, with the ultimate aim of selling his publication.

- In **'Ozymandias'**, Shelley praises the skill of the sculptor in capturing the likeness of the king. The ruler's personality, evident in the inscription, is also clear in the features still visible in the statue's face.

- **'Tissue'** presents the idea of an architect using the power of paper as a recording tool to create a city, layering it and using its transparency as part of its structure.

THEME TRACKER (A01)

Art

- 'My Last Duchess': the Duke's desire for power is clear in his taste in art.

- 'War Photographer': photographs taken to show conflicts to the public are treated as a commodity.

- 'Ozymandias': the sculptor has captured the king's oppressive attitude effectively.

AIMING HIGH: WRITING ABOUT TONE ⭐

In 'War Photographer', Duffy presents the photographer himself as respectful and professional, while implying that others do not take his work as seriously. She also portrays the images themselves as serious and valuable, never actually referring to them as images or photographs, instead using the phrases 'spools of suffering' (2) and 'a hundred agonies' (19). This reminds the reader of the importance of what is in the pictures, rather than any aesthetic qualities they may have, and contributes to a serious and respectful tone.

CONTEXTS

ROMANTICISM

The label 'Romantic', when applied to literature (and other forms of art), does not relate to love and romance, but describes a movement which existed roughly from 1770 to 1850 and was interested in moving away from Classical ideas. This meant that Romantic writers explored nature, the human condition and how people coped with industrialisation. They were also interested in folk and fairy tales – this is the period when the Brothers Grimm began to collect their stories.

Romantic ideals allowed writers to start with inner feelings rather than eternal truths. William Blake's writing fits many of the ideals of Romanticism, and he is now considered a Romantic writer, but he was not part of the movement, whereas Shelley and Wordsworth were consciously and enthusiastically Romantic writers.

TOP TIP (A03)

If a poet was Poet Laureate when they wrote the poem you are studying, think about how that affected their writing.

LAUREATESHIP

The first official Poet Laureate in England was John Dryden, appointed by King Charles II in 1668, although there had been various unofficial Poets Laureate before this. The role is offered by the monarch, and there is traditionally an expectation that the Poet Laureate will provide verse for state occasions such as royal weddings and births, as well as national events such as disasters and celebrations. From 1999, the post became a ten-year one: previously it was held until death. 'The Charge of the Light Brigade' was written during Tennyson's laureateship, and Wordsworth, Hughes and Duffy are or were also Poet Laureate.

INDUSTRIALISATION

The Industrial Revolution took place mostly between the eighteenth and nineteenth centuries in Europe and resulted in cities becoming much larger, dirtier and poorer, although individuals and some organisations accumulated great wealth. Factories were built and conditions for many child and adult labourers worsened since they were no longer working in agriculture but were more likely to be exposed to dangerous chemicals or temperatures and expected to work unreasonable hours. Many of William Blake's poems express his anger about working conditions, especially for children. This is evident in 'London', which explores his concerns about rapid industrialisation and the changes it brought to people's living and working conditions.

THE CRIMEAN WAR

The Crimean War lasted from October 1853 to February 1856 and took place mainly around the Crimean Peninsula and the Black Sea. It was fought initially between Russia and an Allied force consisting of Ottoman, Turkish and Sardinian troops, with Britain and France joining the Allies in 1854. The conflict was mostly about control of the holy places in Jerusalem, which was part of the Ottoman Empire at the time. The Ottoman Sultan allowed the Roman Catholic Church access to churches in Nazareth,

Bethlehem and Jerusalem, and these holy places were also protected by Roman Catholic monks, so attacks on Turkey and the Ottoman Empire by Russia were seen as a threat to the Holy Land. Today, this war is most famous in Britain as the setting of 'The Charge of the Light Brigade' and for the nursing activities of Florence Nightingale and Mary Seacole (see 'Checking Out Me History'). Seacole is now growing in prominence.

Mary Seacole

THE FIRST WORLD WAR

The First World War is well known for its poetry, as there were many soldier poets on the front line: Wilfred Owen, Siegfried Sassoon and Rupert Brooke are some of the best known. Perhaps because postal services and printing were greatly advanced by this war, many more records of soldiers' writing have survived than from earlier conflicts. 'Exposure' is a good example of a late First World War poem expressing the reality of the soldiers' experience on the front line, while 'Bayonet Charge', although written later, was inspired by stories about the First World War Hughes had heard from family members, as well as by his own reading of poetry from the time.

THE BRITISH EMPIRE AND MULTICULTURALISM

The British Empire was established from the late sixteenth to early eighteenth century and comprised countries in India, Africa, the Americas, Australasia and the Caribbean. By 1920 it had become the largest empire in the world and was built upon trading posts and colonies. The modern multicultural society of the United Kingdom has grown out of these links, which were not based on equal power relationships.

AIMING HIGH: COMMENT ON THE SYSTEM ⭐

Agard shows anger towards a system that views his identity as less important than a White British identity. The system seems to view 'de dish ran away with de spoon' (24) as more important than heroes of Caribbean history, perhaps because all the figures he selects are symbols of rebellion. He suggests that it might seem dangerous to the system's self-sustaining power to teach minority children about rebelling against the majority.

MODERN CONFLICTS

While the First and Second World Wars focused mostly on European conflicts, more recent wars have been between Western (USA and European allies) and Middle Eastern forces. In the first Gulf War (1990–1), an Allied force of thirty-four nations led by the USA sought to drive invading Iraqi troops out of Kuwait. The second Gulf War (2003–11) was focused on ending the dictatorship of Saddam Hussein in Iraq. The war in Afghanistan (2001–14) was initiated by a USA invasion of Afghanistan following the 11 September terrorist attacks in the USA in 2001, with an objective of removing the Taliban from power and breaking up the group Al-Qaeda. NATO troops supported the USA in this from 2003.

These wars form the backdrop to some of the later poems in the cluster – 'Poppies', 'War Photographer' and 'Remains' – while 'The Emigrée' seems to refer to a country like Afghanistan where regime change has taken place and people have fled in an attempt to preserve their freedom.

KEY CONTEXT **A03**

Very few of the poems in this cluster refer to religion as a source of power, but where there are specific references, they are worth noting. 'The Charge of the Light Brigade' and 'War Photographer' quote from the Bible, 'London' mentions the Church as a powerful institution, and the Koran appears in 'Tissue' as the place where families' names and details of birth are recorded.

CHECKPOINT 13 **A01**

What is a bayonet?

PROGRESS AND REVISION CHECK

SECTION ONE: CHECK YOUR KNOWLEDGE

Answer these quick questions to test your basic knowledge of the themes and contexts of the poems.

1. In which of these poems is the main theme the power of nature: 'Poppies', 'Storm on the Island', 'Tissue'?

2. In which poem are the main themes memory and nature?

3. In 'My Last Duchess' what theme does Neptune 'taming a sea-horse' signify?

4. In which poem does conflict result in 'spools of suffering'?

5. Which poems treat the theme of being left behind during war?

6. Name four themes relating to power in the cluster.

7. Which poems come from the Romantic period?

8. Which poem has links to industrialisation?

9. Which poem is from the Crimean War?

10. Which poems explore battlefield contexts?

SECTION TWO: CHECK YOUR UNDERSTANDING

Here is a task about a theme in a poem. This requires more thought and a longer response. Try to write at least three to four paragraphs.

Task: How does the poem 'Bayonet Charge' present attitudes to conflict? Think about:

- What happens in the poem
- The soldier's attitude

PROGRESS CHECK

GOOD PROGRESS

I can:

- Explain the main themes and contexts of the poems and how they contribute to the effect on the reader. ☐
- Use a range of appropriate evidence to support any points I make about these elements. ☐

EXCELLENT PROGRESS

I can:

- Analyse in detail the way themes are developed and presented across the poems. ☐
- Refer closely to key aspects of context and the implications they have for the poets' viewpoints, and the interpretation of relationships and ideas. ☐

FORM

What is poetic form?	The physical **structure** of a poem. Usually by form we mean a fixed pattern such as a **sonnet**, ballad or **blank verse**.
Example	In 'My Last Duchess', Browning uses the **dramatic monologue** form, in which he writes entirely in character and in role.
Effect	The Duke's point of view is the only one the reader hears.

DRAMATIC MONOLOGUE

A dramatic monologue is a poem which presents a single speaker as though they are speaking directly to an imagined audience. Often this audience is a specific individual or group, rather than simply the reader of the poem. In 'My Last Duchess', for example, Browning writes as the Duke of Ferrara addressing the servant of a count whose daughter he wishes to marry next.

The dramatic monologue form allows the poet to create a clear character and construct an entertaining scenario to meet their purpose. In this case, Browning wants to comment on the way marriage was often conducted in his time by using this historical reference (the real Duke of Ferrara lived from 1533 to 1598).

Although Browning uses the dramatic monologue form to present us with the Duke's perspective on the Duchess, we are still able to disagree with his judgement on her. This shows how flexible the form is.

KEY QUOTATION: REVEALING THOUGHTS (A02)

Browning's construction of the Duke's character as acutely aware of social position makes him an unpleasant person and an unreliable narrator, meaning the audience is readily able to discount his judgement as flawed. Browning uses complex punctuation and multiple **caesurae** to show his halting speech in 'She thanked men, – good! but thanked / Somehow – I know not how – as if she ranked / My gift of a nine-hundred-years-old name / With anybody's gift.' (31–4) This demonstrates an unsteady thought process and explains his incredulous reaction 'I know not how' (32) to her pleasure at receiving gifts he considers much less valuable than the raising of her social status conferred through marriage.

TOP TIP (A02)

Ensure you have a point to make when commenting on language, form and structure, especially when labelling devices and techniques. It is good to identify 'My Last Duchess' as a dramatic monologue, for example, but it is far better to explore how that makes the Duke powerful in context, as the reader is given only his perspective.

BLANK VERSE

Blank verse is unrhymed iambic pentameter. That is, lines with five 'feet' of two syllables in which the first syllable is unstressed and the second is stressed (de-DUM, like a heartbeat). Poems written in blank verse often do not feel as though they have a regular metre because this rhythm is a natural one for the typical stress patterns of English, so it does not feel intrusive. Many poems which use blank verse do not do so consistently, so there will be occasional lines with eleven or nine syllables and stresses which do not fall exactly on alternate syllables. This can help the metre to feel more natural and not forced, or allow for hesitation and abrupt change.

The poems in this cluster that use blank verse are 'Ozymandias', the extract from 'The Prelude', 'My Last Duchess' and 'Storm on the Island'.

SONNET

A sonnet is a fourteen-line poem, usually written in iambic pentameter. Sonnets have two parts, usually with a different rhyme scheme in each, and traditionally there is a change in meaning or tone around a turning point, which is known as a volta.

There are two main types of sonnet to be found in English, identified by their rhyme schemes. The Italian (or Petrarchan) sonnet consists of two quatrains using *abba* rhymes, followed by a sestet which uses more varied rhymes, but *cdecde*, *cdccdc* or *cdcdcd* are the most common. The Elizabethan sonnet, also often called the Shakespearean sonnet (simply because he wrote so many of them), is formed of three quatrains using alternate rhymes (*abab cdcd efef*) and a closing couplet (*gg*). In an Italian sonnet, the volta comes at the start of the sestet, but the Elizabethan sonnet delays this shift until the couplet at the end.

TOP TIP (A02)

'Ozymandias' is classed as a sonnet although its rhyme scheme does not follow either main pattern in any identifiable way. There is, however, a volta consisting of the strong statement 'Nothing beside remains' (12), as this is the point where the poem's tone shifts and the irony becomes apparent.

STRUCTURE

What is structure?	The organisation of a poem. This may include its construction in terms of stanzas, its order and its use of techniques such as enjambment, caesurae and end-stopping.
Example	In 'Checking Out Me History', Agard uses two different stanza forms to separate 'wha dem want to tell me' (3) from 'me own history' (4).
Effect	The reader can see how the speaker feels differently about the two different kinds of information; this is clear even before we read the detail.

STANZA ORGANISATION

Poets can use stanzas to organise their ideas and give their work direction. Some poems, such as 'London', 'The Emigrée' and 'Exposure', have neat stanzas of a uniform length, with no continuation into the next stanza. Others, such as 'Remains', 'Tissue' and 'The Charge of the Light Brigade', appear uniform at first glance but on closer inspection have a final stanza of a different length to the others, or have stanzas which run into the next. Still others, such as 'My Last Duchess' and 'Storm on the Island', are not broken into stanzas at all. All of these features are potentially worth exploration and comment.

LINE ORGANISATION

What is enjambment?	Continuing a sentence or phrase beyond the end of a line of poetry.
What is caesura?	Using punctuation to create a pause in the middle of a line of poetry; may be used with enjambment to create a natural rhythm.
Example	'Pushed from the shore. It was an act of stealth And troubled pleasure, nor without the voice' (Extract from 'The Prelude', 5–6).
Effect	Using enjambment and caesura works with the blank verse in this poem to create a natural feel to the storytelling. The caesura mimics the pause the speaker experiences after the boat launches into the calm water, while the enjambment gives the voice a confessional quality as the speaker admits his feelings of guilt on the next line, almost as though under his breath.

CHECKPOINT 14 **A02**

How do the six stanzas of 'The Charge of the Light Brigade' divide the story of the poem?

STRUCTURE IN 'WAR PHOTOGRAPHER'

This poem uses a regular stanza organisation, mimicking the photographer's 'ordered rows' (2), and each stanza is **end-stopped**, perhaps suggesting a tight control on the photographer's emotions, which are not allowed to escape too far.

In the second half of the first stanza, Duffy carefully deploys enjambment, caesura and end-stopping to construct an image of the photographer as respectful to his subject. She achieves this by using a religious **semantic field** and comparing the photographer to a priest, but the **enjambment** here gives her the space to expand and explain the image: 'as though this were a church and he / a priest preparing to intone a Mass' (4–5). Then in the next line, she mimics this intoning (reciting words with slight rising and falling of the voice) via a list of war zones – 'Belfast. Beirut. Phnom Penh' (6). Here the full stops provide clear pauses which create a **tone** of respect, just as the priest allows time to think or pray about a subject in church. Finally, this topic is closed with the biblical **allusion** 'All flesh is grass.' (5) which closes the stanza also.

TOP TIP (A02)

Repetition does not only appear at the ends of lines of stanzas. Look at Agard's heavily repetitive use of 'dem tell me' in 'Checking Out Me History'. The many repetitions, combined with the anonymous third **person**, create an accusatory feel.

PATTERNS

Patterns are created in the poems in this cluster in various different ways. **Rhyme** and **rhythm** is one obvious strategy (see page 77 for more detail on these features), but **repetitions** are also an important way of creating patterns and linking different parts of a poem. Two poems that both use repetition to achieve this are 'The Emigrée' and 'Exposure'.

'The Emigrée' closes each stanza with the word 'sunlight', which has the effect of emphasising the idea of hope. The speaker is discussing her enduring memories of her home city, and closing each stanza with this word is a strong way of ensuring that the reader is also left with the clear impression of sunlight above all else.

'Exposure', on the other hand, uses the phrase 'But nothing happens' as a kind of refrain to end most stanzas. This poem is about the loss of hope and presents us with soldiers who are essentially waiting to die of exposure rather than in battle. The repetition here is a reminder that, no matter what, again and again, nothing continues to happen.

RHYME, RHYTHM AND SOUND

What is metre?	The way to describe the **rhythm** of a line of poetry. Metre is defined by the number and type of 'feet' in a line.
Example	'The Charge of the Light Brigade' famously uses **dactylic dimeter** (two dactylic feet – DUM-der-der – per line): 'Half a league, half a league' (1).
Effect	The rhythm creates a sound like horses' hooves galloping.

RHYME

Many of the poems in this cluster use rhyme, but not all do. It is perhaps more noticeable in the older poems, but 'War Photographer' and 'Checking Out Me History' also use rhyme, so it is not entirely true that modern poets avoid it. In 'War Photographer' the rhyme is far less apparent when reading the poem, owing to the natural rhythm and many **enjambments** within the stanzas. This creates less emphasis on the ends of lines than in a poem like 'London', where the rhythm is very distinct, and this is perhaps why the rhyme in Duffy's poem is less obvious.

The rhyme in 'The Charge of the Light Brigade' is effective in presenting the poem's ideas about power and conflict. Tennyson adds emphasis to some lines earlier in the stanzas by rhyming them with the refrain 'six hundred', so the remark 'Some one had blunder'd' (12) is given more importance than it might otherwise have had, and the line 'All the world wonder'd' (52) equally casts doubt on the organisation of the attack. These rhymes allow Tennyson to question those in charge without undermining the sacrifice of the ordinary soldiers. A further set of rhymes also makes clear the soldiers' lack of power in the situation, and highlights their bravery, with the added patterning of the repeated 'Theirs not to make reply, / Theirs not to reason why, / Theirs but to do and die' (13–15).

CHECKPOINT 15 (A02)

What kind of rhyme is used in 'London'?

TOP TIP: WRITING ABOUT RHYTHM AND RHYME (A01)

Be aware that even when there are obvious points to be made about rhyme and rhythm, the most important thing is still to answer the question. Anything you write about rhyme schemes or metre needs to support ideas about how the poet is presenting an aspect of power or conflict in the poem.

SOUND EFFECTS

What is alliteration?	Repetition of consonant sounds, usually at the start of words.
Example	'boundless and bare' ('Ozymandias', 13).
Effect	Repetition of the harsh 'b' sound emphasises the emptiness of the scene.

Alliteration is a useful device for creating sound effects in poetry. **Sibilance** is a special kind of alliteration using 's' sounds, which can be spelt using 's' or 'c'. Owen uses it to great effect in 'Exposure', to create a sense of the sound of bullets shooting through the air: 'Sudden successive flights of bullets streak the silence' (17). This evokes the sound that the soldiers hear, and conveys the suddenness and erratic nature of it effectively for the audience.

DIALECT AND ACCENT

What is dialect?	The specific way people use language because of the social group they belong to or the region they come from. In literature, writing that represents a person's dialect.
Example	Agard uses non-standard spellings and grammar to represent Caribbean pronunciation and word forms: 'Dem tell me / Wha dem want to tell me' ('Checking Out Me History', 2–3). In this case 'dem' is a version of 'them' but 'they' would be used in standard English.
Effect	The speaker's identity as Caribbean is represented in the language as well as in the content of the poem.

Agard writes in a way that represents Caribbean dialect in order to present the speaker's 'own identity' (5) in every way possible within the poem. The poem concerns how the speaker reclaims power by regaining his identity through educating himself, and using authentic language is another way to do this.

LANGUAGE

OVERVIEW

The poems in this cluster offer a range of poetic styles and choices, but all present us with words, phrases and techniques which have been consciously chosen for effect. Exploring what these effects are, in relation to the focus of your question, while showing knowledge of the techniques themselves, is a key way to raise your grade.

VOICE AND VIEWPOINT

What is viewpoint?	The point of view or perspective taken in the poem.
Example	In 'Ozymandias', the speaker is passing on information that they have been given by someone else: 'I met a traveller from an antique land' (1).
Effect	The information is distanced from the reader and adds to the irony of the all-powerful Ozymandias's kingdom being lost and forgotten.

It is worth discussing whether the poems use a first person (I/we) or third person (he/she/it/they) viewpoint, or a combination. In each case, look at how the viewpoint relates to the content or theme of the poem: it will not be enough to say: 'It is first person to be more personal.'

'REMAINS'

Armitage uses an interesting viewpoint in 'Remains'. The poem is written in the first person, but he opens with a plural pronoun 'we' (1) and only shifts to the singular 'I' when he's talking about the impact of seeing the man hit (9). This shows how as a group the soldiers shot the looter, but the speaker experiences the impact of seeing the man's suffering and death on his own.

'KAMIKAZE'

Garland's use of viewpoint is complex, as at first she uses a third person voice. This gives the poem a story-like tone. Later on, however, it switches to the daughter's voice in a more obvious way, using the first person, with italics to show this different voice. Garland even makes the second voice interrupt the first in lines 24–5. This is effective in bringing the story to life, featuring a speaker who is personally affected, and allows Garland to make the daughter question the community's behaviour at the end of the poem.

CHECKPOINT 16 **(A01)**

What is the viewpoint in 'Storm on the Island'?

IMAGERY

What is imagery?	Language used in a non-literal way, i.e. figurative devices such as similes, metaphors and personification.
Example	In the extract from, 'The Prelude', Wordsworth uses the simile 'went heaving through the water like a swan' (20).
Effect	This shows how gracefully the boat moved through the water, as swans are associated with beauty and elegance. It also shows how in tune with nature the speaker was at this point.

> **CHECKPOINT 17** (A02)
>
> What is 'This wizened earth has never troubled us / With hay' ('Storm on the Island', 3–4) an example of?

Imagery and symbolism are key to poetry and are often part of what people instinctively feel makes writing 'poetic'. Similes and metaphors are useful for drawing comparisons with familiar objects or ideas which help readers understand more complex or abstract thoughts. In the poem 'Poppies', Weir is able to convey the idea about the speaker's words being useless in just a few words through a tactile image that fits within her poem's semantic field of textiles. This would not be possible without imagery.

SIMILE

What is a simile?	A comparison made between two objects using 'like' or 'as'.
Example	In 'Storm on the Island', Heaney uses the simile 'spits like a tame cat / Turned savage' (15–16) to express how the sea hits the people's windows.
Effect	This conveys how the usually mild sea transforms into something wild and violent.

'TISSUE'

This poem relies heavily on imagery, exploring what tissue and paper represent and moving from image to image. This lends the poem a dream-like quality, since it becomes far removed from reality. The image 'Fine slips from grocery shops … might fly our lives like paper kites' (21–4) is an interesting presentation of the importance commerce has in our lives. The simile is a tentative one, using the modal verb 'might', but Dharker could be implying that material things and shopping have some kind of control over us, since she seems to be representing our lives as the kites to be flown rather than, as we might expect, the paper slips being the kites.

PERSONIFICATION

What is personification?	Presenting an inanimate object or animal as though it were human.
Example	In the extract from, 'The Prelude', Wordsworth writes that the peak 'upreared its head' (24) and 'strode after me' (29).
Effect	These examples demonstrate how powerless the boy feels, and how much it appears that the peak intends to pursue him.

KEY CONTEXT (A03)

Weir's background as an artist and textiles designer has influenced her choices of imagery in 'Poppies'. She references felting techniques in lines 16–17 to show how the speaker's words become clogged up, tangled or clumped together like woollen fibres matting and turning into a new material.

EXTRACT FROM, 'THE PRELUDE'

Wordsworth moves from imagery to symbolism in this poem, as by the end the 'huge peak' (22) has taken on the significance of a symbol, although it is not clear what it represents. This is part of why it is so disturbing to the speaker: as just a boy, he does not understand his experience fully. Being exposed to the power of nature without being able to comprehend it is unsettling, so the peak might symbolise the mysteries of life.

TOP TIP: BEYOND A CHILD'S COMPREHENSION (A03)

As a Romantic poet, Wordsworth wanted 'The Prelude' to express how his relationship with nature grew and developed into something that was effectively spiritual. The imagery in this section of Book One shows how he, as a boy, begins to shift from noticing the beauty of tiny details to the enormity of the Lake District scenery, but is unable to cope with it at this point in his life.

VOCABULARY CHOICES

What is vocabulary choice?	The precise words chosen by the writer. This choice may be expressed in terms of register, connotation or **semantic field**.
Example	Blake chooses to describe the London streets and the Thames as 'chartered' ('London', 1–2).
Effect	This emphasises his concerns about ownership of land which previously could not be owned privately.

Sometimes we overlook the specific words writers have chosen, thinking that there are no alternatives, but it is important to remember that words are selected, often very carefully indeed, for their particular meanings and values. In the final version of the poem, there may well seem not to be possible alternatives precisely because the words chosen work so well.

In 'War Photographer', Duffy uses 'intone' (5) rather than 'recite' or 'chant' as her **verb** of choice for what the priest does with the Mass. This is much more effective at evoking the ritualistic behaviour and degree of respect the photographer displays.

REGISTER

What is register?	The level of language – whether it is formal or informal, standard or **colloquial**.
Example	In 'Remains', Armitage chooses to use a low register, giving the poem a colloquial tone: 'one of them legs it up the road' (3).
Effect	This conveys the real-life nature of the scenario he is presenting.

Armitage's choice of a colloquial register in 'Remains' is effective, as we see how the soldier's everyday life is affected by his experience. The poem is full of conversational phrases which create a sense of the speaker telling us his thoughts directly, as well as the feeling of a well-rehearsed **anecdote** that he has been over many times.

KEY QUOTATION: MULTIPLE MEANINGS (A02)

Armitage closes his poem with particularly rich examples of colloquial speech, using the idiomatic phrase 'near to the knuckle' (29), which means on the borders of acceptable, and the phrase 'his bloody life in my bloody hands' (30). Here Armitage combines colloquialism with **imagery** by using a mild swear word to convey the soldier's anger as he holds the man's life in his hands – both literally and **metaphorically**.

CHECKPOINT 18 (A02)

What makes 'merciless' an effective choice to describe the 'iced east winds' (1) in 'Exposure'?

CONNOTATIONS

What are connotations?	The set of values or associations that a word has, in addition to its main dictionary definition.
Example	When Hughes uses the phrase 'he lugged a rifle numb as a smashed arm' ('Bayonet Charge', 6), 'lugged' implies a lack of care.
Effect	This emphasises the soldier's loss of concentration and focus.

Hughes's choice of 'lugged', as well as having connotations of carelessness, is also of a relatively low register, which adds to the sense of the soldier's lack of respect for his rifle.

SEMANTIC FIELD

What is a semantic field?	A collection of words which are related by belonging to the same category.
Example	In 'Poppies', Weir uses several words from a semantic field related to textiles: see lines 6, 17, 28 and 34.
Effect	This helps to pull the poem together by relating the images to one another.

In the example above, Weir creates a secondary theme of texture and textiles running through her poem. A semantic field can also help to create a metaphor that relates more closely to the poem's theme or message, as in Heaney's use in 'Storm on the Island' of a violent semantic field which escalates from 'pummels' (10) to 'dives' (13), 'strafes' (17) and 'bombarded' (18). Another strong example is Duffy's use of a church-related semantic field to convey the photographer's respect for his material in 'War Photographer'.

⭐ AIMING HIGH: AMBIGUITY

Ambiguity – the lack of one definite meaning – can be a deliberate device employed by a poet. Obscuring meaning, or allowing space for different interpretations can be part of the effect a poet wants to create in a poem, using unreliable memories or confused events to add impact, even to deliberately 'play' with the reader's understanding of a situation. For example, in the extract from, 'The Prelude', it is not clear exactly what it is about the great mountain by the lake that terrifies the speaker and causes him to be troubled by the encounter even after the event. In fact, Wordsworth suggests that it is the ambiguity of the peak itself that is so troubling: 'my brain worked with a dim and undetermined sense / Of unknown modes of being' (35–7). The speaker is unable to communicate the source of his fear, but his emotions come across strongly and we share in his confusion. Similarly, in 'Poppies', it is unclear whether the speaker's son is still alive or has died, but the sense of loss in the poem is heightened by the ambiguity as we are drawn into the emotions of the mother.

CHECKPOINT 19 (A01)

What are the connotations of Weir's choice of 'steeled' in 'steeled the softening of my face' ('Poppies, 10–11)?

TONE AND MOOD

What is tone?	The atmosphere or feeling evoked by a poem.
Example	'London' has a rather sad tone overall, but reaches a peak in the middle two stanzas, where it is angrier.
Effect	The reader's emotions are engaged through those of the speaker.

A poem's tone and mood are created by all its language, form and structure techniques working together. As seen in the example above, the overall mood of a poem may shift, but usually not very dramatically.

TOP TIP (A01)

Challenge yourself to use effective adjectives to describe the tone or mood of the texts you are studying. Working with a thesaurus may help you to delineate fine shades of 'positive', 'negative', 'happy' or 'tense' moods. This will also be useful for analysing extracts from longer texts.

POSITIVE POEMS

Arguably the poems in this cluster with the most positive moods are 'The Charge of the Light Brigade' and 'Checking Out Me History'. Both are celebratory poems, but in quite different ways. 'The Charge of the Light Brigade' seeks to celebrate the nobility and bravery of a specific brigade who were mostly killed in battle. Tennyson does this through a very strong dactylic rhythm, frequent rhymes and highly charged positive language such as 'honour' and 'noble' (53–5). Although 'Checking Out Me History' is also celebrating specific historical figures, it is doing so to celebrate Black British identity. Agard achieves this through dialect words such as 'dem' and 'bout' (6), a structure which separates Caribbean and British history, and strong use of rhyme. It is interesting that these very different poems have these aspects in common.

REVISION FOCUS: COMPARING MOOD

Choose three poems that you feel have different negative moods. Challenge yourself by choosing poems that you do not feel are similar.

Draw up a table with four columns headed, 'Name of poem', 'Point about mood', 'Example/evidence', 'Explanation/detail', and three rows.

Name of poem	Point about mood	Example/ evidence	Explanation/ detail

Fill in the table using one row for each of your three poems and see if you notice anything surprising.

PROGRESS AND REVISION CHECK

SECTION ONE: CHECK YOUR KNOWLEDGE

Answer these quick questions to test your basic knowledge of the language, form and structure of the poems.

1. Which poem is a sonnet, and what is unusual about it?
2. Who speaks in a low register, and in which poem?
3. In which poem is a 'huge peak' personified?
4. In which poem does the image 'mind-forged manacles' occur and what does it refer to?
5. In what metre is 'The Charge of the Light Brigade' written?
6. What does a caesura do?
7. What language technique is used in 'Checking Out Me History'?
8. Which poem uses repetition of 'But nothing happens'?
9. What is a dramatic monologue?
10. In which poem does the image of 'paper kites' appear, and what might they represent?

SECTION TWO: CHECK YOUR UNDERSTANDING

Here is a task about a poetic techniques. This requires more thought and a longer response. Try to write at least three to four paragraphs.

Task: How does Seamus Heaney show that nature can be powerful in 'Storm on the Island'? Think about:

- What poetic techniques the poet uses
- What effects are created through these techniques

PROGRESS CHECK

GOOD PROGRESS

I can:

- Explain how the poets use key poetic techniques to shape events, show relationships and develop ideas. ☐
- Use relevant quotations to support the points I make, and refer to the effect of some techniques. ☐

EXCELLENT PROGRESS

I can:

- Analyse in detail the poets' use of particular techniques to convey ideas, create a voice or viewpoint and evoke mood or setting. ☐
- Select from a range of evidence, including apt quotations, to infer the effect of particular techniques and to develop wider interpretations. ☐

THE EXAM

In **Section B** of the exam you will be given one poem (printed on the exam paper) from the *Power and Conflict* cluster and asked to compare it with another poem from the cluster, of your own choice.

So, what sorts of things might you be asked to compare/contrast between poems? Here are three possibilities:

- Attitudes towards war
- Power of nature
- Effects of power on people

HOW WOULD THIS WORK FOR A GIVEN POEM?

TOP TIP (A01)

Remember to separate your points into clear paragraphs.

A typical question might be:

Compare how poets present memories of conflict in 'Remains' and in one other poem from *Power and Conflict*.

WHAT POSSIBLE POEMS COULD 'REMAINS' BE COMPARED WITH?

The examiners are looking for you to be able to draw links with any poem in the cluster – not just to revise a particular few – and that will be part of the skill you demonstrate, but there will be certain poems that are more closely linked in content to the given poem than others. For example, in this case:

- 'War Photographer' – both poems are about not being able to forget
- 'The Charge of the Light Brigade' – to contrast national remembrance with more personal memories
- The extract from, 'The Prelude' – to compare the after-effects of a single moment on the mind

HOW WOULD THIS RELATE TO ASSESSMENT OBJECTIVES 1, 2 AND 3?

In 'War Photographer', for example, the writer:

AO1

- Shows how the photographer remembers the context of the photographs that he is developing
- Compares the photographer's home with the places he has visited for work

AO2

- Uses sentence structure to form contrasts between 'then' and 'now'
- Uses listing to show how the memories pile up

AO3

- References specific conflicts to remind the reader about them
- Implies publication in a broadsheet newspaper

LINKS BETWEEN POEMS

As stated on the previous page, theoretically you should be ready to compare/contrast the given poem with any other poem in the cluster, but it might be useful to prepare a few combinations. Here are some possible links:

Poem	Thematic or contextual links	Voice or formal/structural links
'Ozymandias'	'My Last Duchess' also presents ideas about **social control**: both Ozymandias and the Duke proudly protect their power.	'Ozymandias' uses a distanced **third** person **speaker**, while 'My Last Duchess' is a dramatic monologue providing the Duke's voice first hand.
'London'	Like 'Checking Out Me History', 'London' shows awareness of the **oppression** of different social groups, but is from the **eighteenth century**, while 'Checking Out Me History' is **contemporary**.	'London' uses a very measured and regular rhythm and rhyme scheme; 'Checking Out Me History' uses two different **stanza layouts** to present the different social groups it features.
Extract from, 'The Prelude'	Like 'Remains', this extract explores the effects of one moment on the mind, but 'The Prelude' is strongly influenced by its context of **Romanticism**.	Both use a **first person** viewpoint, but the voice in 'Remains' is more modern and colloquial.
'My Last Duchess'	'London' also criticises the structures and system of **social class**.	'London' openly criticises the class system using an 'outsider' viewpoint; the Duke's voice relies on the reader to infer Browning's criticism.
'The Charge of the Light Brigade'	Like 'Exposure', this poem explores the catastrophic **effects of war** upon individual soldiers.	Both make strong use of repetition and **sound patterning**.
'Exposure'	'Bayonet Charge' also presents a soldier's **First World War** experience, but was written later and not from **personal experience**.	'Exposure' uses a more formal **stanza structure**; the more modern 'Bayonet Charge' employs more enjambment and less repetition and rhyme.
'Storm on the Island'	The extract from 'The Prelude' also explores the power of nature.	Both use a **first person voice**; neither is broken into **stanzas**.

continued on page 88

'Bayonet Charge'	Like 'Kamikaze', this focuses on **one moment** in wartime, but 'Bayonet Charge' describes what happens around that moment whereas 'Kamikaze' explores the **impact** of that moment on the rest of the pilot's life.	Both poems use a **third person viewpoint**, but 'Kamikaze' uses words and phrases that create a storytelling atmosphere while 'Bayonet Charge' has a more condensed style, using harsher **sound techniques** as well as imagery to create its effects.
'Remains'	'War Photographer' also explores the **effects of conflict**, but while 'Remains' focuses on the devastating effects on the soldier, 'War Photographer' focuses on the lack of effect on the public, and how the photographer feels about this.	'Remains' uses **enjambment** between the stanzas; 'War Photographer' uses end-stopping.
'Poppies'	Like 'Exposure', this explores ideas about **family and home** in the context of conflict. While 'Poppies' presents a mother's thoughts on her son's departure for war, 'Exposure' features the soldiers' yearning for home.	While both have a **first person speaker**, 'Poppies' uses direct address to include the son.
'War Photographer'	Like 'The Charge of the Light Brigade', this is concerned with **how the public reacts to conflict**.	Both use a **third person viewpoint**, but in 'The Charge of the Light Brigade' the tone is celebratory while in 'War Photographer' it is resigned.
'Tissue'	'Poppies' is also about **memory**, but 'Tissue' explores this in terms of records.	Both use imagery related to texture and layering.
'The Emigrée'	Like 'Checking Out Me History', this explores ideas about **resisting** the **abuse of power**.	'Checking Out Me History' uses distinct **stanza** layouts and dialect; 'The Émigrée' uses vivid **imagery**.
'Checking Out Me History'	Like 'Ozymandias', this shows a **decline of power**, but this is explicit in 'Ozymandias', while 'Checking Out Me History' describes how power is reclaimed.	Both poems use form to highlight meaning: 'Ozymandias' is a sonnet which deviates from traditional forms; 'Checking Out Me History' uses two different **stanza layouts** to separate British and Caribbean culture.
'Kamikaze'	Like 'Remains', this shows the **impact of one moment** on a person's life, although in 'Remains' this event is in the recent past.	'Remains' uses a strong **first person voice**, while 'Kamikaze' mostly uses a **third person speaker** to evoke a story-like tone.

EXPLORING IDEAS AND ISSUES IN BOTH POEMS

The main focus for the exam question will be some sort of issue, idea or attitude related to the overall theme of power and conflict. So, how might you respond to this? You might explore connections related to:

1 The **context and background** of the issue. For example, is there a tradition for poetry about how power is controlled in society? If so, how might the issue have been dealt with differently over time? What seems to be the attitude to it in your two poems? What are the political issues connected with it?

Example: Read this student's paragraph about one poem in relation to social power:

> Poetry can be used to raise awareness about an issue. In 'Checking Out Me History', Agard seeks to highlight how one kind of power has led to a group of people not being familiar with their own history. He does this by contrasting what 'Dem tell me' – some of which can be seen as unimportant and not helpful, or in some cases not even historical fact, such as 'Robin Hood' – with what 'dem never tell me bout'.

REVISION FOCUS: EFFECTS OF CONFLICT

Choose two poems which deal with the effects of conflict, and make a diagram (a mind map, table or other diagram) comparing and contrasting these effects, focusing on the contexts of the poems.

2 The **voice**, **viewpoint** and **perspective** of each speaker and how they are similar or different. For example, is a particular speaker writing 'in the moment', whilst the other is reflecting from a distance or at an older age? Does one poem use more formal language, while the other is written more **colloquially**? Do the poems address the reader directly, or do they relate to the audience in different ways?

Example: Read one student's paragraph about their chosen second poem in relation to power in 'Ozymandias':

> In 'My Last Duchess', the speaker, like Ozymandias, sees himself as-all powerful. He tells the imagined audience 'I choose / Never to stoop.' This shows the Duke's sense of his own power over his wife, and his faith in the social hierarchy of Ferrara, in which his position is secure.

3 The **language and literary techniques/effects** in the two poems. This is a large area, but drawing out what is distinctively similar or different, perhaps in the degree of imagery, the directness of language or semantic fields, will enable you to explore parallels and divisions. For example, the colloquial language of 'Remains' could be compared with the more formal, grandiose language of 'The Charge of the Light Brigade'.

Example: Here a student comments on the effect of imagery in 'Exposure' and in 'Bayonet Charge':

Soldiers' physical experience on the battlefield is explored in different ways using imagery in both 'Exposure' and 'Bayonet Charge'. In the first, Owen uses personification to show the effect of the snow, which he describes as 'Pale flakes with fingering stealth' which 'come feeling for our faces', characterising the snow as a criminal seeking to harm the soldiers. In 'Bayonet Charge', however, Hughes's imagery is disturbing in a different way, as it has less sense of deliberate malice. Here the soldier feels the sensation of a 'patriotic tear that had brimmed in his eye / Sweating like molten iron from the centre of his chest', which creates an impression of patriotism turned to pain.

4 The **form**, **structure** and **patterning** of the poems. Looking at how the poems are divided and their structural characteristics will enable you to draw out key links and differences: for example, by commenting on repetitions of particular words or phrases, or how a line is shortened, broken or repeated for effect.

Example: Here a student demonstrates real insight in contrasting the effect of stanza organisation, end-stopping and enjambment in each poem.

In 'War Photographer', Duffy presents an image of the photographer organising his images 'in ordered rows'. This organisation is mirrored in the neat, end-stopped stanzas she presents us with, perhaps suggesting that despite the photographer's memories intruding upon his developing work, his professionalism and experience allow him to contain his emotional reactions and continue working to 'do what someone must'.

However in 'Remains' we see how Armitage allows most stanzas to flow into one another using enjambment, just as the soldier's mind constantly chases the memory of the shot looter. This repetitious thinking is echoed in the repeated ideas, revisited in different phrases throughout the poem as Armitage demonstrates the intrusive nature of the memories that 'the drink and the drugs won't flush ... out'. Both poets therefore use stanza organisation to support the points they make about memories of conflict in their poems but in different ways.

Remember, it is not enough simply to 'feature spot' or write about what you know or have learned about the two poems. You need to relate your knowledge to the **specific focus** of the task.

THE LANGUAGE OF EXPLORATION, COMPARISON AND CONTRAST

You are probably familiar with the range of useful connectives and other words or phrases that can help you to explain ideas, draw links or explore contrasts in your responses, but here is a grid containing some key terms. Bear in mind that these are just as useful for developing an argument about one poem as they are for two.

Sequencing ideas	Developing an idea	Illustrating	Cause and effect
firstly, to start with, initially secondly, next, then, later finally, in conclusion	as well as and also too furthermore moreover in addition	for example such as for instance as shown by in this way	so because therefore thus hence consequently as a result of leading to
Comparing similarities	**Qualifying**	**Contrasting**	**Emphasising**
both equally in the same way similarly likewise as	however yet although unless except if apart from despite	in contrast on the other hand whereas instead of alternatively otherwise unlike	indeed notably above all especially particularly most of all

REVISION FOCUS: EXPLORATION, COMPARISON AND CONTRAST

Go back to the student paragraphs on pages 89 and 90. Can you spot any of the key terms above being used? Could you replace any with alternatives from the grid?

PROGRESS CHECK

GOOD PROGRESS

I can:
- Recognise and explain clearly similarities and differences between the two poems. ☐
- Justify my comments with relevant evidence and accurate terminology. ☐

EXCELLENT PROGRESS

I can:
- Interpret the poets' methods and approaches to draw out insights about the two poems. ☐
- Select apt and precise evidence to support my points and use subject terminology thoughtfully. ☐

THE EXAM

As well as the questions based on the *Power and Conflict* cluster of poems from the Anthology you have been given, you will also have to answer questions in the exam on two **new** poems which you haven't seen before. This is often referred to as the 'unseen' element of the exam, and it comes in **Section C**, after you have answered the question on the poems from the Anthology cluster (in **Section B**).

In **Section C**, you will be:

- given an 'unseen' poem printed in the exam paper
- asked to answer a single essay question on this poem (worth 24 marks), focused on how the poet presents certain ideas
- given a second 'unseen' poem (also printed on your exam paper)
- asked to answer a comparative question based on links between the second and first poem (worth 8 marks).

So, you will have **two** 'unseen' poems to answer on, with most of the available marks for your response to the first unseen poem, rather than the comparison.

ASSESSMENT

This part of the exam assesses **Assessment Objective 1** (response to ideas, supported by evidence) and **Assessment Objective 2** (writers' effects – language, form and structure) equally, with 50% of the marks for each.

QUESTION TYPES

The **first question** will ask you something about the way the poet presents particular ideas, for example:

'How does the poet present the speaker's feelings about his father?' or 'How does the poet present ideas about the power of nature?'

The **second question** will ask you to compare the first and second poem in some way, for example:

'In both poems the speakers describe feelings about leaving home. What are the similarities and/or differences between the ways the poets present those feelings?'

TYPES OR STYLES OF POEM

There is no one set style or predictable 'type' of poem you will be given, so you need to prepare for every eventuality. However, part of the skills being assessed is your ability to recognise what is **distinctive** about the poem, what the poet is saying, and how he or she says it – its flavour, if you like – and the ingredients that make up the recipe.

TOP TIP (A01)

The total marks for these two questions is **32**, which is slightly more than for the Section B question on the cluster, so make sure you give **at least the same amount of time**, if not slightly more, for the 'unseens' – so, **at least 45 minutes**.

HOW TO APPROACH THE FIRST 'UNSEEN' POEM QUESTION

It is perfectly normal to see an 'unseen' poem as a blur of words on the page, and feel it's a difficult puzzle, like an equation, you have to solve. However, it doesn't need to be like this! It is important that you:

- approach the poem with an **open mind**, looking to **enjoy exploring its language and ideas**
- have some **key strategies** ready which you can quickly put into action
- stick to **time limits for note-making** and **annotations** and leave yourself enough time to write your answer.

STAGE 1: READ THE POEM AND THE QUESTION

- Read the poem **once through** without making notes, just to make sense of it.
- Keep the **focus of the question** in the back of your mind – this will give you a clue to the poem's **main theme** and the **angle** you need to explore.

STAGE 2: MAKE NOTES AND ANNOTATIONS ON THE PAGE

- Go back over the poem, noting the things which stood out to you as you read, always focusing on the **question**.
- Think about how the poem 'speaks' to you – what kind of voice and viewpoint are being used?
- Look at how the poet is using **language**; what are the key techniques?
- What about structure and **patterns** – how is the poem put together and how does that support the **theme**?

For **Stage 2** of the process, once you have read the first poem through without note-making, you need to read it a second time, this time exploring it in detail and at the same time keeping an eye on the 'bigger picture'.

STAGE 3: USE YOUR NOTES AND ANNOTATIONS TO HELP YOU WRITE YOUR RESPONSE

- Make sure you mention the question's **focus** as quickly as possible, to help you focus on the right things straight away and not wander into a general summary of the poem.
- Have a plan of action, perhaps starting with 'big picture' ideas such as **voice** and **viewpoint** before moving into discussing finer details.
- Address the poem's use of **language** by unpicking **quotations** and explaining their **effects**, as well as using **terminology** when you can.
- Explore the poem's **structure** and use of **patterns** with reference to how these relate to the **ideas** in the question.

Turn over the page to find an example question with the **key words** highlighted. (Remember that the task will come after the poem on the actual paper.)

> **TOP TIP** (A01)
>
> Try to spend **30 to 35 minutes** on the **first question.** This should be enough for you to read, make notes and respond.

Question: How does the poet present the **speaker's feelings** about his **loved one** in this poem?

This suggests you should be looking for:

● a **viewpoint** or **emotions** about the loved one
● **positive** or **negative language** or **descriptions**
● what **sort of 'story'** if any is told about the relationship and **what is happening/has happened.**

Now look at how the 'unseen' poem has been annotated:

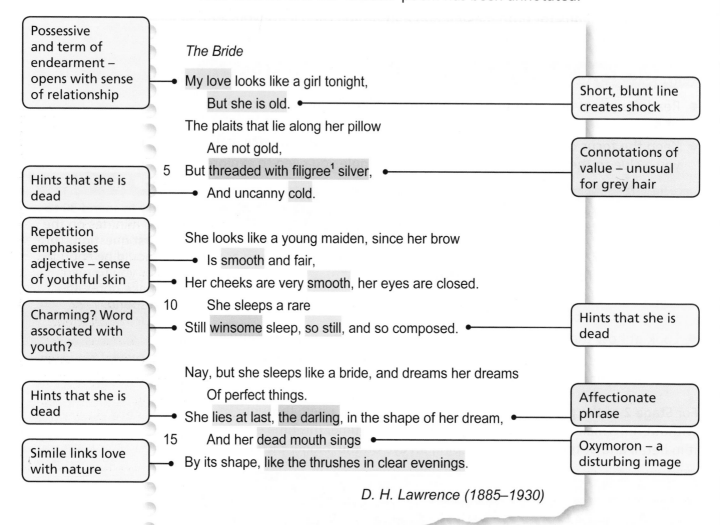

Possessive and term of endearment – opens with sense of relationship

Hints that she is dead

Repetition emphasises adjective – sense of youthful skin

Charming? Word associated with youth?

Hints that she is dead

Simile links love with nature

The Bride

My love looks like a girl tonight,
     But she is old.
The plaits that lie along her pillow
     Are not gold,
5   But threaded with filigree[1] silver,
     And uncanny cold.

She looks like a young maiden, since her brow
     Is smooth and fair,
Her cheeks are very smooth, her eyes are closed.
10   She sleeps a rare
Still winsome sleep, so still, and so composed.

Nay, but she sleeps like a bride, and dreams her dreams
     Of perfect things.
She lies at last, the darling, in the shape of her dream,
15   And her dead mouth sings
By its shape, like the thrushes in clear evenings.

D. H. Lawrence (1885–1930)

Short, blunt line creates shock

Connotations of value – unusual for grey hair

Hints that she is dead

Affectionate phrase

Oxymoron – a disturbing image

[1] filigree = fine, ornamental wire

WHAT ARE THE OVERALL CONCLUSIONS?

For higher marks examiners will be looking to see if you can arrive at a 'conceptualisation' – a sort of complete picture of the poem – which you can explain consistently.

For example, based on his/her annotations, the student might say that:

The woman in the poem is presented as loved and valued by the speaker; she at first appears to be sleeping peacefully, but is in fact dead. This disturbing central idea is balanced by the sense that she is so at peace that her face appears youthful once more.

WRITING A RESPONSE

Here is one possible way of structuring your response:

Paragraph	Point
Opening paragraph	Establish quickly and clearly the 'story' the poem tells. For example: *The speaker in 'The Bride' describes his love as 'like a girl' although he immediately tells us 'she is old' and it soon becomes apparent that she is dead. In death, she is at peace and associated with nature.*
Paragraphs 2–4	Introduce detailed points related to 'the speaker's feelings': • the main feeling shown is love and belonging: 'my love', 'bride' – affectionate and genuine • he sees her as valuable: 'silver filigree' – presented here positively • he is happy that she is at peace: 'she lies at last, the darling'.
Paragraphs 5–6	Add a couple of further ideas: • death has returned her to a youthful state: 'smooth' cheeks • she is aligned with nature: 'her dead mouth sings … like the thrushes in clear evenings' – simile links her to end-of-day birdsong • tone is unsettling owing to contradicting language such as 'dead mouth songs'.
Concluding paragraph	Sum up concisely – don't list all the ideas again. For example: *D. H. Lawrence's poem tenderly praises the loved one who has passed away. The speaker's feelings of love and affection for her are made clear as he praises her beauty, but there is also a tone of sadness and loss. She is preserved in death almost as though she is alive, which heightens the sense of loss and melancholy. There is almost something supernatural about the woman who is dead but looks as though she is only sleeping, that adds to the 'uncanny' atmosphere and suggests the speaker may be in a dream-like state himself.*

HOW TO APPROACH THE SECOND 'UNSEEN' POEM QUESTION

You have fewer marks for the comparison question, so:

- Read through the second poem and, with the question task in mind, make very brief notes around it (perhaps 2 minutes of quick annotation).
- Decide the main points of comparison and difference.
- Write your response.

Try to allow **15 to 20 minutes** for this, the **second question**. Your teacher may advise you to spend more or less time on the first 'unseen' and Anthology cluster questions depending on your own strengths and weaknesses, so make sure you check what their advice is too.

TOP TIP (A01)

For further help with comparing poems, turn to **Part Five** of this Study Guide. This section gives advice on comparing poems in the Anthology cluster, but you can apply the same skills when comparing 'unseen' poems too.

PRACTICE TASK 1

Now, complete this two-part practice task featuring two new 'unseen' poems, using the process on pages 92–5. Write two full-length responses and then use the **Mark scheme** on pages 118–19 to assess your work.

> **Question 1:** How does the poet present ideas about nature in this poem? (24 marks)

1 Underline the key words in the title.

2 Read the poem through once, without making notes but with the focus of the task in the back of your mind.

3 Read it again, making notes, adding annotations or highlighting.

4 Write your response.

Patroling Barnegat

Wild, wild the storm, and the sea high running
Steady the roar of the gale, with incessant undertone muttering,
Shouts of demoniac laughter fitfully piercing and pealing,
Waves, air, midnight, their savagest trinity lashing,
5   Out in the shadows there milk-white combs careering,
On beachy slush and sand spirts of snow fierce slanting,
Where through the murk the easterly death-wind breasting,
Through cutting swirl and spray watchful and firm advancing,
(That in the distance! is that a wreck? is the red signal flaring?)
10   Slush and sand of the beach tireless till daylight wending,
Steadily, slowly, through hoarse roar never remitting,
Along the midnight edge by those milk-white combs careering,
A group of dim, weird forms, struggling, the night confronting,
That savage trinity warily watching.

Walt Whitman (1819–92)

Now read the second poem:

> *The Night is Darkening Round Me*
>
> The night is darkening round me,
> The wild winds coldly blow;
> But a tyrant spell has bound me,
> And I cannot, cannot go.
>
> 5   The giant trees are bending
> Their bare boughs weighed with snow;
> The storm is fast descending,
> And yet I cannot go.
>
> Clouds beyond clouds above me,
> 10   Wastes beyond wastes below;
> But nothing drear¹ can move me;
> I will not, cannot go.
>
> *Emily Brontë (1818–48)*

Glossary

¹ drear = dreary

> **Question 2:** In both poems, 'Patroling Barnegat' and 'The Night is Darkening Round Me', the speakers discuss the impact of nature on humankind. What are the similarities/differences between the ways the poets present these ideas? (8 marks)

1 Quickly read the second poem and second question, and make very brief notes.

2 Write your comparison – three to four paragraphs on similarities and one on differences.

PRACTICE TASK 2

Now complete this further 'unseen' two-part practice task. Write two full-length responses and then use the Mark scheme on pages 118–19 to assess your work.

> **Question 1:** How does the poet present ideas about memory and the past in this poem? (24 marks)

I Remember, I Remember

I remember, I remember
The house where I was born,
The little window where the sun
Came peeping in at morn;
5   He never came a wink too soon
Nor brought too long a day;
But now, I often wish the night
Had borne my breath away.

I remember, I remember
10   The roses red and white,
The violets and the lily cups—
Those flowers made of light!
The lilacs where the robin built,
And where my brother set
15   The laburnum on his birthday,—
The tree is living yet!

I remember, I remember
Where I was used to swing,
And thought the air must rush as fresh
20   To swallows on the wing;
My spirit flew in feathers then
That is so heavy now,
The summer pools could hardly cool
The fever on my brow.

25   I remember, I remember
The fir-trees dark and high;
I used to think their slender tops
Were close against the sky:
It was a childish ignorance,
30   But now 'tis little joy
To know I'm farther off from Heaven
Than when I was a boy.

Thomas Hood (1799–1845)

Piano

Softly, in the dusk, a woman is singing to me;
Taking me back down the vista of years, till I see
A child sitting under the piano, in the boom of the tingling strings
And pressing the small, poised feet of a mother who smiles as she sings.

5   In spite of myself, the insidious mastery of song
Betrays me back, till the heart of me weeps to belong
To the old Sunday evenings at home, with winter outside
And hymns in the cosy parlour, the tinkling piano our guide.

So now it is vain for the singer to burst into clamour
10 With the great black piano appassionato. The glamour
Of childish days is upon me, my manhood is cast
Down in the flood of remembrance, I weep like a child for the past.

D. H. Lawrence (1885–1930)

Question 2: In both poems, 'I Remember, I Remember' and 'The Piano', the speakers remember what it was like to be a child. What are the similarities/differences between the ways the poets present ideas about childhood? (8 marks)

PROGRESS CHECK ✓

GOOD PROGRESS

I can:

● Explain the methods of the writer of the first 'unseen' poem clearly using a range of references. ☐

● Recognise and explain clearly similarities and differences between the two 'unseen' poems. ☐

EXCELLENT PROGRESS

I can:

● Draw out and interpret the methods and approaches of the writer of the first 'unseen' poem, selecting apt and precise evidence. ☐

● Make a convincing comparison between the two 'unseen' poems, with well-judged analysis. ☐

UNDERSTANDING THE QUESTION

TOP TIP **(A01)**

This section (**Part Seven**) of the Study Guide gives you help and advice on approaching **Section B** of the exam where the **Anthology cluster** is examined. Advice on **Section C: Unseen poems** is provided in **Part Six**.

In **Section B** of the exam, you will:

● be given **one poem from the cluster**, which will be **printed on your exam paper**

and

● be asked to **compare it** with **another poem of your choice** from the cluster, by answering one **question** on an **aspect common** to the **given poem** and the **one of your choice**.

The question is worth **30 marks**, and examines **AO1**, **AO2** and **AO3**, with **80%** of marks available for **AO1 and AO2**. This does not mean you should ignore **AO3** (contextual factors or perspectives) but do not write too much about it! You will have approximately **45 minutes** to answer the question.

TYPICAL QUESTIONS

In your exam, a typical question will look like this, with a focus on power and/or conflict:

> **Question:** Compare how poets present ideas about power in 'London' and one other poem from the cluster you have studied.

BREAK DOWN THE QUESTION

Pick out the key words or phrases. For example:

Compare how poets **present ideas about power** in **'London'** and one other **poem** from the cluster you have studied.

What does this tell you?

● You need to focus on ideas about power in 'London' and another poem, making links between them.

● You should analyse how those ideas are presented by writing about the language and techniques the poets use.

PLANNING YOUR ANSWER

Bearing in mind that you have just 45 minutes (or less if you want to spend more time on **Section A** or **C**), you will need to respond swiftly and efficiently. This means that you should spend no more than **5 minutes** planning – remember, you will already know the poems well.

STAGE 1: SELECTING POEMS FOR COMPARISON

Your teacher may have already suggested possible poems to compare 'London' with but here are a few ideas.

● 'My Last Duchess' – hierarchy and social class
● 'Checking Out Me History' – social control and resistance
● 'Ozymandias' – hierarchy and traditional power/social class

STAGE 2: ANNOTATING THE GIVEN POEM AND CREATING LINKS

Look at how one student has used the exam paper to annotate the poem, and make notes in red on the second, 'Ozymandias'.

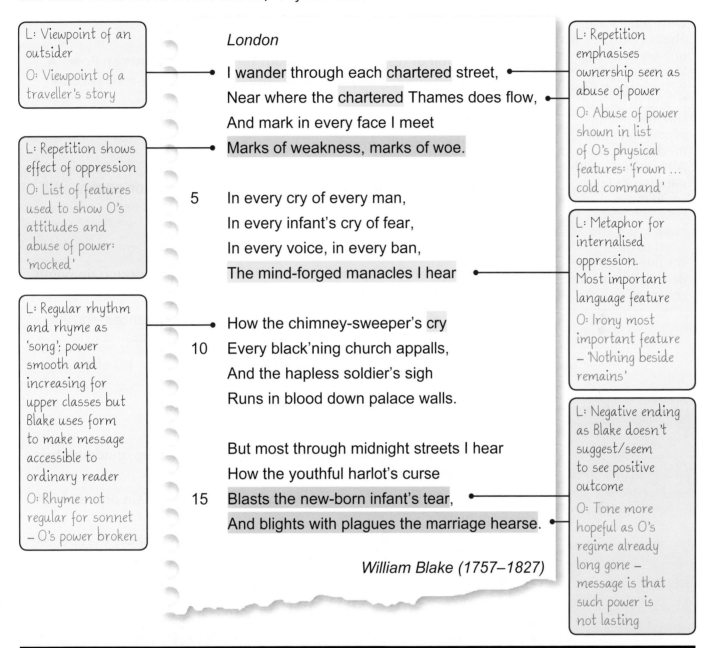

L: Viewpoint of an outsider

O: Viewpoint of a traveller's story

L: Repetition shows effect of oppression

O: List of features used to show O's attitudes and abuse of power: 'mocked'

L: Regular rhythm and rhyme as 'song'; power smooth and increasing for upper classes but Blake uses form to make message accessible to ordinary reader

O: Rhyme not regular for sonnet – O's power broken

London

I wander through each chartered street,
Near where the chartered Thames does flow,
And mark in every face I meet
Marks of weakness, marks of woe.

5   In every cry of every man,
In every infant's cry of fear,
In every voice, in every ban,
The mind-forged manacles I hear

How the chimney-sweeper's cry
10 Every black'ning church appalls,
And the hapless soldier's sigh
Runs in blood down palace walls.

But most through midnight streets I hear
How the youthful harlot's curse
15 Blasts the new-born infant's tear,
And blights with plagues the marriage hearse.

William Blake (1757–1827)

L: Repetition emphasises ownership seen as abuse of power

O: Abuse of power shown in list of O's physical features: 'frown ... cold command'

L: Metaphor for internalised oppression. Most important language feature

O: Irony most important feature – 'Nothing beside remains'

L: Negative ending as Blake doesn't suggest/seem to see positive outcome

O: Tone more hopeful as O's regime already long gone – message is that such power is not lasting

Key things to compare	Key things to contrast
Institutions and empires oppress individuals – church/chimney-sweeper; Ozymandias 'mocked'	Ozymandias's power destroyed – non-conformist rhyme reflects this; Blake writes accessibly for ordinary readers through smooth, regular rhythm and rhyme of song form
Outsider viewpoint – 'I wander' vs 'traveller'	
Abuse of power shown (but in different ways – repetition or list of features)	Tone: 'London' more negative
Romantic context	Use of language: Blake – imagery; Shelley – irony.
Symbolism: black – corruption, blood shed for palace; statue of Ozymandias as power metaphorically crumbled	

STAGE 3: WRITING YOUR RESPONSE

You may not have time to write a detailed plan, but this is one suggested structure for your response, which involves writing about the first poem, then bringing in the second, but making a clear link to the first when you do so.

First section of response: write about **three or four points** on **Poem A**, perhaps on voice, viewpoint and **context**, supported by reference to the **language**:

- Blake uses an outsider viewpoint – although it is first person the speaker is not involved.
- Blake shows how institutions oppress individuals.
- Repetition is used to show the effects of oppression on all the people.

Second section of response: bring in **Poem B**, perhaps picking up points of **similarity** and **difference**:

- Shelley also uses an outsider viewpoint with the distanced 'traveller'.
- Shelley shows how Ozymandias is presented as a tyrant.
- Shelley lists Ozymandias's features but does not show his effect on others directly.

Third section of response: one or two points **developing** or **adding to** earlier ideas on **either of the two poems**:

- Each poet uses different techniques to make their main points about power.
- Blake uses metaphor – 'mind-forged manacles' – to show that people have internalised their oppression.
- Shelley uses irony to emphasise Ozymandias's lack of long-term power.

Final section: concluding paragraph drawing points together, ideally making a point about **each poem as a whole**:

- The tone of each is different owing to their different messages: Blake is more negative as he is commenting on a current inbalance of power; Shelley can be more positive as he is showing past power and how in the end all empires fall.

RESPONDING TO WRITERS' EFFECTS

The two most important assessment objectives are **AO1** and **AO2**. They are about *what* poets do (the choices they make, and the effects these create), *what* your ideas are (your analysis and interpretation) and *how* you write about them (how well you explain your ideas).

ASSESSMENT OBJECTIVE 1

What does it say?	What does it mean?	Dos and don'ts
Read, understand and respond to texts. Students should be able to: ● Maintain a critical style and develop an informed personal response ● Use textual references, including quotations, to support and illustrate interpretations	You must: ● Use some of the literary terms you have learned (correctly!) ● Write in a professional way (not a sloppy, chatty way) ● Show that you have thought for yourself ● Back up your ideas with examples, including quotations	**Don't write:** *The Light Brigade must have been scared. Tennyson uses frightening words to describe their situation.* **Do write:** *Tennyson's description of the Light Brigade's situation makes the reader feel sympathy for them as they rode 'into the valley of Death'. Tennyson encourages us to hear the cannon as they 'volley'd and thunder'd'.*

IMPROVING YOUR CRITICAL STYLE

Use a variety of words and phrases to show effects:

The poet *suggests ..., conveys ..., implies ..., presents how ..., explores ..., demonstrates ..., describes how ..., shows how ...*
I/we (as readers) *infer ..., recognise ..., understand ..., question ..., see ..., are given ..., reflect ...*

For example, look at these two alternative paragraphs by different students about 'The Charge of the Light Brigade'. Note the difference in the quality of expression.

Student A:

> This makes it seem as if Tennyson is speaking

Alfred Lord Tennyson says that the Light Brigade are nice and good soldiers. He writes 'boldly they rode and well'. This shows that they are good and brave and did not hesitate to go into battle. This shows that they were brave even though they knew they might die and did not have much power in the situation. Tennyson is saying that bravery is very important.

> Chatty and informal

> Repetitive – better to use an alternative

> Vague

Student B:

Fits with the idea of the overall way the Light Brigade is shown

Tennyson presents the Light Brigade as noble, brave and virtuous soldiers when they ride into battle. They demonstrate their honourable attitude towards battle when Tennyson describes them using the phrase 'Boldly they rode and well'. The adverbs 'boldly' and 'well' imply that they ignored concerns about personal safety to do the work required of them. Tennyson also seems to be suggesting that despite their possible anxiety about the battle, they had faith, since he repeats the biblical phrase 'Into the valley of Death'.

Clear and precise language

Good variety of vocabulary

Looks beyond the obvious and infers meaning with personal interpretation

Phrase allows the student to explore the idea rather than state it as fact

ASSESSMENT OBJECTIVE 2 (A02)

What does it say?	What does it mean?	Dos and don'ts
Analyse the language, form and structure used by the poet to create meanings and effects, using relevant subject terminology where appropriate.	'Analyse' – comment **in detail** on **particular aspects** of the poem or language. 'Language' – vocabulary, imagery, variety of sentences, speech, etc. 'Form' – **how** the poem is put together (e.g. dramatic monologue, sonnet, stanza construction, etc.) 'Structure' – the **order** in which events or information are presented, patterns or repetitions such as rhyme or rhythm, etc. 'Create meaning' – what can we, as readers, **infer** from what the poet tells us? What is **implied** by particular descriptions, or events? 'Subject terminology' – **words** you should use when writing about poetry, such as viewpoint, imagery, **stanza**, **metre**, etc.	**Don't write:** *The writing is really descriptive in this poem so you could really imagine the cavalry charging down into the valley.* **Do write:** *Tennyson **conveys** the sense in which the valley **setting** contributes to the disaster as the Light Brigade become trapped between the 'cannon to right of them' and 'cannon to left of them'. The reader can almost hear the horses' hooves in the **metre** and then see the sabres 'flash' and hear the cannon.*

IMPLICATIONS, INFERENCES AND INTERPRETATIONS

- The best analysis focuses on specific ideas or events, or uses of language and thinks about what is **implied**.
- This means drawing **inferences**. On the surface, Tennyson's description of the battle is a celebration of the troops' bravery, but how much is it also a comment on the behaviour of the commanders?
- From the inferences you make across the poem as a whole, you can arrive at your own **interpretation** – a sense of the bigger picture, a wider evaluation of a speaker, relationship or idea.

USING QUOTATIONS

One of the secrets of success in writing exam essays is to use quotations **effectively**. There are five basic principles:

1 Quote only what is most useful.

2 Do not use a quotation that repeats what you have just written.

3 Put quotation marks, e.g. ' ', around the quotation.

4 Write the quotation exactly as it appears in the original.

5 Use the quotation so that it fits neatly into your sentence.

EXAM FOCUS: USING QUOTATIONS **A01**

Quotations should be used to develop the line of thought in your essay, and to 'zoom in' on key details, such as language choices. The **mid-level** example below shows a clear and effective way of doing this:

| Makes a clear point | Wordsworth presents the peak as blocking the boy's earlier pleasure in rowing. The boy says that it 'Towered up between me and the stars'. | Gives an apt quotation |

Explains the effect of the quotation — Wordsworth shows the reader that the peak immediately affects the boy's experience and spoils his enjoyment.

However, really **high-level responses** will go further. They will make an even more precise point, support it with an even more appropriate quotation, focus on particular words and phrases and explain the effect or what is implied to make a wider point or draw inferences. Here is an example:

Precise point

Precise quotation

Explanation/ implication/effect

Wordsworth shows that the peak physically separates the boy from his experience with nature. The boy says that 'the grim shape / Towered up between me and the stars'. The word 'towered' conveys to the reader the size of the barrier between himself and the light from the stars that he was earlier enjoying. Through the boy's positive experience with nature at the start of the poem, Wordsworth shows the reader that the boy desires a relationship with nature, but this is compromised after the experience with the 'huge peak'.

Language feature

Further development/link

ANNOTATED SAMPLE ANSWERS

This section provides three sample responses, one at a **mid** level, one at a **good** level, and one at a **very high** level.

> **Question:** Compare how poets present ideas about conflict in 'Exposure' and one other poem from the collection you have studied.

SAMPLE ANSWER 1

'Exposure' and 'Bayonet Charge' are quite similar because both are based on the First World War, although Wilfred Owen was writing in the war and Ted Hughes didn't have personal experience of it but was writing from family stories about it and from reading Owen's and others' poetry. This means that they both present some ideas which are the same about conflict.

AO3 — Good brief comparison of contexts

'Exposure' mostly presents negative ideas about conflict, showing how the soldiers are suffering in the trenches. Owen writes about how they are all freezing, like when he says 'Our brains ache, in the merciless iced east winds that knive us'. This shows how the soldiers are cold because the wind feels like a knife cutting into them. Owen presents an unexpected side of conflict, how the soldiers are suffering because they are waiting and waiting in the freezing cold for something to happen.

AO2 — Basic explanation of the effect but could discuss language chosen

AO1 — Too informal and sounds as if he is speaking

'Bayonet Charge', on the other hand, shows action in conflict as it presents the moment when the soldier races forwards. There is stillness here too, and Hughes uses a simile of the soldier's foot being like 'statuary' when he's stuck because he doesn't want to charge, but seeing a hare thrashing about dying reminds the soldier how dangerous it is to be out in the open and he goes back to charging like he's supposed to.

AO1 — Good embedded and short quotation

AO2 — Valid use of terminology but lacks discussion of effect

AO1 — Knows the poem but summarises rather than interpreting or discussing

'Exposure' shows the soldiers' frustration with conflict, how they are fed up with waiting. Owen uses the repeated phrase 'But nothing happens' at the end of several stanzas to emphasise this. Putting it at the end of the stanzas makes it like a refrain so it is more memorable, and the repetition shows that the soldiers keep expecting something to happen but it never does.

AO1 — Too informal

AO2 — Useful comment on structure

AO2 — Interprets effect of repetition

A01 This point is not tightly focused on the poem

A lot of what is described in 'Exposure' isn't really about the conflict, although it is because of the conflict that the soldiers are experiencing it. We hear a bit about bullets and the barbed wire but mostly it is about the weather, not the conflict. 'Bayonet Charge' is actually about the fighting, though, so the poem is more about the conflict itself.

A01 Clear point in a topic sentence for this paragraph

A03 Shows knowledge of context but gives far too much information

In 'Bayonet Charge', the soldier forgets what he's fighting for in the end and just wants to get to safety. Hughes shows that the soldier drops all the ideas of what he is supposed to be fighting for when he charges. He shows this in the quote 'King, honour, human dignity, etcetera'. At the start of the First World War everyone was told it would be an honour to fight in it and women would give white feathers to men who were the right age and weren't fighting to say they were cowards because it was shameful not to be a soldier. At the time of the start of the war everyone believed it was for honour and glory but by the end it was obvious that it was a mess and a waste and thousands of men had died for pretty much nothing. Owen's poem shows how the soldiers were frustrated and Hughes's poem shows that 'honour' and 'human dignity' don't really have anything to do with war.

A03 Links poems to context

Both 'Exposure' and 'Bayonet Charge' are based on the First World War and show negative views about it, but Owen writes more about the general conditions and Hughes about the actual fighting.

MID LEVEL

Comment

Some good points about context hidden among too much historical information and occasional valid points on how the poets present conflict using language and structure. However, the style is often too chatty and informal and needs to refer more to language techniques and devices.

For a Good Level:

- Use a more formal and critical style and avoid chatty, informal words and phrases.
- Always embed quotations into sentences.
- Avoid summarising poems.
- Be cautious about explaining context. If you explain history rather than discuss the text, this will be too much information.

SAMPLE ANSWER 2

AO1 Good to name other poem right away, but a little more on how they differ would be better.

'Exposure' and 'The Charge of the Light Brigade' present different ideas about conflict. Owen wrote 'Exposure' from his actual experience in the First World War trenches, while Tennyson was writing from the point of view of someone not involved in the Crimean War, so these contrasting contexts are part of the reason for their ideas being so unalike..

AO3 Good overview of key contextual difference between poems

AO1 Relevant terminology

Owen's presentation of conflict in 'Exposure' is that 'nothing happens', but the soldiers are still dying of 'Exposure'. The repetition of the phrase 'But nothing happens' shows us that the soldiers just keep experiencing nothing after nothing, like they are waiting and waiting. He does describe some fighting, but it seems to be far away: 'the flickering gunnery rumbles, / Far off', so the main idea about conflict shown in this poem is that it is boring and involves a lot of waiting in dangerous conditions.

AO1 Well-embedded quotation

AO1 Focused on question

AO2 Explanation of effect of feature – this could be more in depth

AO1 Weak vocabulary

AO3 Clear focus on question and link to other poem

Tennyson's presentation of conflict in 'The Charge of the Light Brigade' is quite different, as it is all about the action of the battlefield. Tennyson also uses repetition, but he uses it to show movement and to create pace, as well as to remind the reader to admire the 'six hundred'. The famous opening, 'Half a league, half a league / Half a league onward' sets up the dactylic dimeter which mimics the sound of horses' hooves, presenting a grand impression of conflict.

AO2 Good explanation of effect also making a comparative point

AO2 Explains effect of feature but not how this links to conflict

AO1 Good use of terminology

Owen also uses sound techniques to present ideas about conflict. There is quite a lot of alliteration and especially sibilance in 'Exposure'. For example the line 'Sudden successive flights of bullets streak the silence' contributes to his presentation of conflict by creating the sound of the bullets through the soft sibilant sounds. Owen doesn't let us think about conflict as action-packed for long, however, as the next line says that the bullets are 'Less deadly than the air that shudders black with snow', making clear once again that the conditions are the most dangerous thing the men face.

AO1 Links to previous paragraph

AO2 Effect of feature

AO2 Extended explanation

A03 Apt link to context

There is a tone of bitterness to 'Exposure', which is understandable in a poem of the late First World War written by a soldier who had suffered and seen others suffer and die. Even the environment is seen as an enemy in the image 'Dawn massing in the east her melancholy army' which personifies the dawn as leader of an army with 'ranks on shivering ranks of grey' and makes it sound as though the dawn is deliberately planning how to attack the soldiers. Owen uses the poem's tone to present conflict as exhausting and perhaps ultimately pointless.

A02 Effective explanation with embedded quotation

A01 Interpretation could be more developed

The tone of 'The Charge of the Light Brigade', on the other hand, is often seen as glorifying war, with its semantic field of honour: 'noble six hundred!', 'honour the charge they made!'. Conflict in this poem is presented with religious words as 'Hell' and 'the valley of Death', but because the men fighting are celebrated, and he describes the fighting in heroic terms like 'flash'd all their sabres bare', many read the poem as a glorification of conflict. Tennyson really wants to point out that 'some one had blunder'd', though, and shows the soldiers' lack of power in the situation by repeating 'Theirs not to', and he shows how brave they are by also repeating 'Into the valley of Death' so the poem can also be seen as a celebration of them in spite of the possible pointlessness of the actual battle.

A01 Good use of terminology

A01 Careful phrasing to show possible interpretation – but a very long sentence

A01 Repetitive phrasing

A01 Point fully supported and developed – but another very long sentence

Overall, 'Exposure' is a much bleaker poem, which is perhaps because of its context. 'The Charge of the Light Brigade' was written to commemorate the soldiers who died at the Battle of Balaclava, while Owen's motivation for writing was to express much more personal feelings about conflict.

A01 Conclusion returns to point from introduction, making essay well rounded

GOOD LEVEL

Comment

There are some strong points made about how the poets present conflict, and some good links to the poems' contexts. Some features are commented on in some depth, showing good analytical skills, while others could be further developed. Expression is clear and at times effective but there are places where it could be stronger.

For a High Level:

- Use more sophisticated expression and try to avoid repetitive phrasing.
- Focus on literary techniques and devices that you can link to the question.
- Embed all quotations.

SAMPLE ANSWER 3

A01 Addresses question immediately

A01 Labelled device

The ideas about conflict shown in 'Exposure' are overwhelmingly depressing. Owen paints a picture of the First World War as endless, treacherous and deadly – not through battle, but lack of protection from the 'merciless iced east winds'. Here, Owen uses sibilance to recreate the sounds of the winds hissing through the trenches, and the adjective 'merciless' to add personification and characterise them as having evil intent.

A01 Embedded quotation

A02 Detailed explanation of effect including analysis of single word with a further label

A03 Compares poems' contexts briefly

A01 Useful comment on whole structure of poem

'Remains' is about a more recent conflict, presenting a different kind of warfare. Here a soldier in a more urban context describes the after-effects of an incident. In Armitage's poem, it's not only the context of conflict itself that is difficult to bear, but the psychological impact after the event. One of the key ways he presents this is through the use of repetitive content, phrased in different ways. For example, in the second stanza, Armitage finds four different ways to express that three of them were responsible, from listing: 'myself and somebody else and somebody else', to insisting on their similarities with the cliché 'three of a kind'. This repetition mirrors the way the incident repeats itself endlessly in the soldier's mind. It is also worthy of note that up to this point in the poem, the viewpoint is plural first person, as the three of them are acting together to shoot the looter, but after this, when the focus shifts to the effects of this incident on the soldier, the viewpoint is singular first person. Although the soldier shares responsibility for the killing itself, the psychological after-effects are his alone.

A02 Detailed description of effect of feature

Both poets make effective use of military-based imagery to enable the reader to understand their views about conflict. Owen reverses a well-known symbol of hope to present the dawn as an enemy 'massing in the east her melancholy army', which continues the pattern established in the first line with 'merciless' to give the impression of the entire environment trying to kill the soldiers. Armitage uses the standard military phrase 'dug in behind enemy lines' metaphorically, to describe the profound invasion of the memory in the soldier's head. Using military imagery implies that he feels ambushed by images of the dead man, and also that he cannot escape the war, even once he is back at home.

A02 Detailed feature – not just imagery, but pattern of imagery

A01 Link to earlier point to show knowledge of overview

There are also key differences in the ways the poets present conflict, however. Owen uses half-rhyme throughout 'Exposure' with lines 1 and 4 and 2 and 3 almost rhyming, e.g. 'knive us' and 'nervous'. These half-rhymes imply a lack of closure, just as the soldiers 'know war lasts', or doesn't end, we the readers are made to know that poetry doesn't end neatly with nice tidy rhymes.

A02 Detailed comment on effect of feature

A03 Brief mention of poem as contemporary shows knowledge of context

Armitage doesn't use any kind of rhyme in 'Remains', as a contemporary poem, but he does use colloquial language and a considerable amount of idiom. The overall effect is that the soldier is telling his story directly to us, and also that this is a story that he has told many times, like a well-worn anecdote that he is unable to get past. Opening with 'On another occasion' implies that the soldier tells many war anecdotes and that this is just one of many – at least to start with. Words and phrases such as 'So' and 'End of story' give a strongly conversational tone to the poem, creating the impression that it is being told to us, rather than written down. The final two-line stanza is also highly idiomatic, with the phrase 'near to the knuckle' and 'his bloody life in my bloody hands'. The idiom 'near to the knuckle' suggests that it is all too much for the soldier, and the final line is a pun, with the suggestion of swearing as well as the meaning of the man's life being in the soldier's hands because he is responsible for his death. This jokey tone can be seen as typical of soldier banter, perhaps avoiding presenting too serious an attitude to events. This is arguably common in veterans of conflict, who often downplay any sense of heroism or personal suffering. Armitage's choices of clipped and colloquial phrasing hide the profound emotions actually felt.

A01 Labelled technique

A02 Excellent analysis

A03 Wider evaluation of the effects of conflict

A03 Compares poems' contexts

In conclusion, the key similarities between these poems are in their attitude to conflict: that it ruins lives. They both show this using imagery which borrows military terms, but most of the techniques they use are quite different, perhaps partially because of the context in which they were writing. Unlike Owen, whose poem was written at the Front, Armitage was writing at a distance, not least because he is not the soldier himself, but also because the speaker in his poem is removed from immediate physical danger.

VERY HIGH LEVEL

Comment

This is an excellent response showing a strong understanding of both poems, and of how to produce a convincing poetry response. It is fluent and articulate and links both poems well, drawing effectively on their contexts in both poetic and historical terms. Literary features are analysed closely, and a range of points are made effectively.

PRACTICE TASK 3

Write a full-length response to this exam-style question and then use the

> **Question:** Compare how poets present ideas about conflict in 'War Photographer' and one other poem from the cluster you have studied.

STAGE 1

Mark scheme on pages 118–19 to assess your response.
Read the given poem and choose a second poem to write about:

- Find the given poem in your Anthology and read it carefully. Underline any key words or phrases you may want to pick out and make some quick notes on the key themes.
- Now choose a poem to compare it with. Is there a poem that discusses a similar issue or deals with the same theme in a contrasting way?

STAGE 2

- For some suggestions for linked poems, see the grid on pages 87–8.

Plan your points and write your response:

- Plan quickly and efficiently by using key words from the question.
- Write equally about the given poem and the other poem you have chosen.
- Explore key points of comparison in terms of content, poetic forms and language, and context.
- Focus on the techniques the poets use and the effect of these on the reader.
- Offer your own interpretations, insights and thoughts on the poems,

STAGE 3

  where possible.
- Support your ideas with relevant evidence, including quotations.

Check your response!

Once you've written your draft, use the **Mark scheme** on pages 118–19 to check your response. Here you'll find a list of points you could have made – these are just suggestions but if you think you have missed something important, try to add it into your response in your own words. You can also use the **General skills** section on page 120 to remind you of the key criteria and to check your skills.

TOP TIP (A01)

Remember to choose your comparison poem carefully. 'War Photographer' covers conflict in several different ways, so the linked poem you choose will decide which angle you make most important. Which angle is most important to you? Which possible linked poem are you most comfortable with?

LITERARY TERMS

adjective	a word that describes a noun, making it more precise
adverb	a word that describes a verb, showing (for example) how, when or where the action happens
alliteration	repetition of the same consonant sound in words close to one another
allusion	reference to something from another text
anecdote	story about something that happened to a person
archetype	a symbol that recurs throughout a culture
assonance	when the same vowel sound appears in the same place in a series of words
blank verse	unrhymed iambic pentameter
caesura	a pause in the middle of a line, marked by punctuation
colloquial	language which is informal or everyday in nature
conditional phrase	a phrase expressing what might happen if certain conditions are met
connective	a word or phrase that joins clauses, sentences or paragraphs together
dactylic dimeter	a rhythm of two feet per line made up of a stressed beat followed by two unstressed beats (DUM-der-der, DUM-de-der)
dialect	accent and vocabulary, varying by region and social background
direct address	'speaking' directly to an audience
discourse marker	a word or phrase used to change the topic, or return to an earlier topic
dramatic monologue	a poem written 'in character' using a single voice and taking place in one scene
end-stopping	finishing off a line of poetry with punctuation
enjambment	running a line of poetry into the next line
epic	a long poem form that relates a heroic story, usually a quest
figurative language	using imagery to write in a non-literal way
form	the type of poem, e.g. sonnet, dramatic monologue
half-rhyme	words which almost rhyme; also called near rhyme
iambic pentameter	a rhythm of five feet per line made up of an unstressed beat followed by a stressed one (da-DUM, repeated five times)

imagery	figurative language, or similes, metaphors, personification
internal rhyme	a rhyme within a line of poetry
irony	words intended to mean the opposite of what they appear to say
juxtaposition	placing clashing or contrasting ideas next to one another
metaphor	a figure of speech in which something is described as being something else
modal verb	an auxiliary verb expressing possibility, probability, certainty or permission: can, could, shall, should, will, would, may, might, must
noun	a word naming a person, place or object, or something abstract, such as an idea or belief
onomatopoeia	words that sound like the noise they describe
pentameter	a line with five metric 'feet'
person	a poem may use a viewpoint described as either 'first person' (I, we) or 'third person' (he, she, they, it) or, rarely, 'second person' (you)
personification	a figure of speech giving human qualities to inanimate objects or animals
pronoun	a word standing for a noun: I, me, he, him, etc.
repetition	repeating a word or phrase for effect
rhyme	words which rhyme end in the same sound
rhyming couplets	a pair of lines which rhyme and come one after another in a poem
rhythm	the 'beat' of a poem
semantic field	a group of words which belong to the same category, e.g. bullet, knife, bomb
sibilance	alliteration with only 's' and soft 'c' sounds
simile	a figure of speech describing something as being 'like' or 'as' something else
sonnet	a poetic form having fourteen lines, a particular rhyme scheme, and a volta
structure	the way a text is organised
tense	the grammatical time frame a text is presented in – past, present or future
tone	the emotional atmosphere conveyed by a text overall, or at a particular point
verb	a word which expresses an action, state or process
viewpoint	the perspective of a poem: the person who is telling it
vocabulary choice	the words chosen by the poet to produce a specific effect
voice	related to viewpoint, the perspective created by the poet
volta	a turning point in a sonnet

CHECKPOINT ANSWERS

CHECKPOINT 1, page 10

Face

CHECKPOINT 2, page 17

Stealth

CHECKPOINT 3, page 21

Roman god of the sea

CHECKPOINT 4, page 25

To mimic cannon fire at regular intervals throughout the poem.

CHECKPOINT 5, page 29

Personification

CHECKPOINT 6, page 32

Adjectives

CHECKPOINT 7, page 41

It seems to create disorder by interrupting the existing pattern of things.

CHECKPOINT 8, page 44

They have all been war zones.

CHECKPOINT 9, page 52

It seems to have been taken over by a dictatorship and/or affected by civil war.

CHECKPOINT 10, page 55

He assumes that, like the speaker in the poem, readers will not know about them already, but will be familiar with the figures from British culture.

CHECKPOINT 11, page 62

The monarchy

CHECKPOINT 12, page 67

'Storm on the Island'

CHECKPOINT 13, page 71

A blade attached to the end of a rifle

CHECKPOINT 14, page 75

They separate the stages of the battle: introducing the brigade, the instruction to charge, entering the valley, the battle itself, leaving the valley, a final comment.

CHECKPOINT 15, page 77

Alternate rhyme (*abab*)

CHECKPOINT 16, page 79

A plural first person – possibly the whole community, or a household or family

CHECKPOINT 17, page 80

Personification

CHECKPOINT 18, page 82

It conveys that the winds keep on going, but also implies that they could choose not to or know that they are hurting the soldiers but do it anyway, even though they are aware of the pain they are causing. It personifies them at the same time as mercy (or lack of it) is a human trait.

CHECKPOINT 19, page 83

It makes it sound impenetrable, as if she is putting on a fixed mask that nothing could get through.

PROGRESS AND REVISION CHECK ANSWERS

PART TWO, PAGES 60–1

Section One

1. Jane Weir
2. 'Checking Out Me History'
3. 'Bayonet Charge'
4. An emigrée has left a country, an immigrant has come into a country
5. Ozymandias
6. Russians and Cossacks
7. Family history, 'names and histories'
8. 'My Last Duchess'
9. 'Storm on the Island'
10. 'The Charge of the Light Brigade'
11. The war photographer
12. Church, palace
13. Dropping of daylight; bough of cherries; white mule
14. London
15. Legs, face/visage, lip, hand, heart
16. 'Bayonet Charge'
17. Nothing
18. A 'huge peak'
19. Mackerel, crabs, prawns, whitebait, tuna
20. 'Remains'

Section Two

Task 1:

- Clash of war interrupting life shown in poppies attached to clothing (4–6)
- Physical sensations of the speaker described to show mother–son relationship and mother's feelings: (9–10)
- Semantic field of textiles used to create metaphor of anxiety: (27–8)
- Final image of dove contrasts freedom of son: (33–4)

Task 2:

- Dactylic dimeter mimics sound and rhythm of horses galloping: 'Half a league, half a league' (1)
- Repetition to show sheer number of cannon: 'Cannon to right of them, / Cannon to left of them, / Cannon in front of them' (18–20)
- Repetition to create tension: 'Into the valley of Death' (7)
- Sense of noise and chaos: 'Volley'd and thunder'd' (42)

PART THREE, PAGE 72

Section One

1. 'Storm on the Island'
2. 'The Prelude'
3. Art
4. 'War Photographer'
5. 'Poppies', 'The Charge of the Light Brigade', 'War Photographer', 'Kamikaze'
6. Social control, responsibility, resisting oppression, social structures
7. 'Ozymandias', 'London', 'The Prelude'
8. 'London'
9. 'The Charge of the Light Brigade'
10. 'The Charge of the Light Brigade', 'Exposure', 'Bayonet Charge'

Section Two

- Confusion of the battlefield shown in **imagery**: 'dazzled with rifle fire' (4)
- Suddenly changing attitude in the face of actual conflict shown through **simile**: 'patriotic tear … sweating like molten iron from the centre of his chest' (5–6)
- Idea of conflict as making unreasonable demands on troops shown in soldier's confusion: 'foot hung like / Statuary in mid-stride' (14–15)
- Reality of battlefield not like grand ideals of attitudes to conflict: 'King, honour, human dignity, etcetera / Dropped like luxuries' (20–1)

PART FOUR, PAGE 85

Section One

1. 'Ozymandias'; it does not follow either the Elizabethan or the Italian/ Petrarchan rhyme scheme
2. The soldier in 'Remains'
3. Extract from, 'The Prelude'
4. 'London'; the people's internalised oppression
5. Dactylic dimeter
6. Creates a pause within a line
7. Dialect
8. 'Exposure'
9. A poem written in a single person's voice like a speech from a play
10. 'Tissue'; our lives

Section Two

- **Personification** of the earth: 'never troubled us / With hay' (3–4)
- Escalation of attack through the poem: 'pummels' (10), 'flung' (14), 'strafes' (17) to 'bombarded' (18)
- Imagery that presents nature as living and spiteful: simile 'spits like a tame cat / Turned savage' (15–16)
- Military **metaphors** imply nature plans an attack: 'wind dives / And strafes' (16–17)

MARK SCHEME

PRACTICE TASK 1, PAGE 96

Question 1 – 'Patroling Barnegat'

Points you could have made:

- Use of present tense verbs
- Use of listing structure and stanza form
- Third-person and distant viewpoint
- Violent, wild imagery

Question 2 – Comparison points

Points you could have made:

- Attitudes to the power of the storms: 'The Night is Darkening Round Me' focuses on the effect on the speaker, seeming to embrace and welcome the 'tyrant' power of the storm, while 'Patroling Barnegat' is more distanced, reflecting the storm's power but not in any personal sense
- Different uses of viewpoint with a first-person perspective in 'The Night is Darkening Round Me'
- Similarities in imagery and tone with violence depicted in both poems
- Differences in use of structure and form

PRACTICE TASK 2, PAGE 98–9

Question 1 – 'I Remember, I Remember'

Points you could have made:

- the strongly personal first person voice reflects on the past ('the house where I was born') and contrasts childhood joy with current sadness – even wishing, it seems, for death in the last two lines of the first verse.
- the repetition of 'remember' from the start, and as the first line of each stanza, focuses the reader's attention on a range of childhood memories. Then, in each verse these past memories are juxtaposed with the present through the use of tense forms ('where I *was* born' and 'I often *wish*') and comparatives such as 'now', 'than' and 'yet', all indicating a change of view.
- the poet's use of sound is also notable in the regular rhymes (2nd and 4th; 6th and 8th lines) which are broken up by unrhymed pairs of lines to undercut the sing-song nature of the verse, matching the bitter-sweet mood.
- the poet presents positive images of the past: the sun personified as a friendly visitor ('peeping in'); the colourful roses; the 'light' lilies indicating youth and life; and by implication a different sort of 'lightness' as alluded to by 'my spirit flew in feathers', suggesting the airy freedom of birds contrasted with the burden of age – 'that is so heavy now.'

- also, ideas related to childish innocence and joy – the childish swing where the speaker compared himself to a swallow; the belief that the 'tree-tops' were almost touching the sky – are brought to an abrupt end by the weight of experience, suggesting that the speaker has not lived life as he should have done, and is now 'farther off from Heaven' than when a child.

Question 2 – Comparison points

Points you could have made:

- both poems deal with the idea of childhood being a place of joy and comfort, and how readily these ideas can be brought to mind: Lawrence's ideas are evoked by the immediate experience of hearing a woman sing, but Hood's are ongoing memories.

- Lawrence explores the idea of how children relate to the adult world, focusing in on vivid, physical detail through the senses – the 'boom of the tingling strings' of a piano, the 'pressing' of the 'small, poised feet' of his mother – so that the speaker's past life is brought more sharply into focus. Hood's evocation of childhood shows how the natural world creates lasting impressions – sun, flowers, robin, swallows, fir-trees.

- Hood suggests childhood is untroubled and regrets the loss of innocence. It represents a sort of perfection, which conjures up spiritual ideas about a lost Eden. Lawrence's vision of childhood is more homely in its description of the 'cosy parlour', though it too is perfect in a different way – having a sort of 'glamour'. He perhaps implies his idea of childhood may be rose-tinted and that the poem is more a comment on the power of music to stir emotion – almost wickedly – hence the use of words like 'insidious' and 'betrays', as it is about a desire to be a child again.

PRACTICE TASK 3, PAGE 112

Points you could have made:

- Attitudes to conflict: respectful attitude of photographer himself contrasted with the public's
- Conflict between war zones and home in England – how Duffy presents England
- Use of stanza structures, rhyme scheme and tone
- Possible comparisons with 'Exposure', 'The Charge of the Light Brigade' or 'Kamikaze' in terms of attitudes to conflict
- Third-person viewpoint – imagined character – possible comparisons with 'Bayonet Charge' or 'Poppies'
- Comparison with 'Remains', 'The Charge of the Light Brigade', 'Exposure' or 'Bayonet Charge' in terms of being in a war zone, but contrast drawn for actual role there

Now use the table on page 120 to make a judgement about the level of your response.

GENERAL SKILLS

Make a judgement about your level based on the points you made in response to Practice tasks 1 and 2 and the skills you showed:

Level	Key elements	Writing skills	Tick your level
Very high	**Very well-structured answer which gives a rounded and convincing viewpoint.** You use very detailed analysis of the poets' methods and effects on the reader, using precise references which are fluently woven into what you say. You draw inferences, consider more than one perspective or angle, including the context where relevant, and make interpretations about the poems as a whole.	You spell and punctuate with consistent accuracy, and use a very wide range of vocabulary and sentence structures to achieve effective control of meaning.	
Good to High	**A thoughtful, detailed response with well-chosen references.** At the top end, you address all aspects of the task in a clearly expressed way, and examine key aspects and poetic techniques in detail. You are beginning to consider implications, explore alternative interpretations or ideas; you do this fairly regularly and with some confidence.	You spell and punctuate with considerable accuracy, and use a considerable range of vocabulary and sentence structures to achieve general control of meaning.	
Mid	**A consistent response with clear understanding of the main ideas shown.** You use a range of references to support your ideas and your viewpoint is logical and easy to follow. Some evidence of commenting on writers' effects and poetic techniques, though more needed.	You spell and punctuate with reasonable accuracy, and use a reasonable range of vocabulary and sentence structures.	
Lower	**Some relevant ideas but an inconsistent and rather simple response in places.** You show you have understood the task and you make some points to support what you say, but the evidence is not always well chosen. Your analysis is a bit basic and you do not comment in much detail on the poets' methods.	Your spelling and punctuation is inconsistent and your vocabulary and sentence structures are both limited. Some of these make your meaning unclear.	